Legal Research
Using the Internet

The West Legal Studies Series

Your options keep growing with West Legal Studies

Each year our list continues to offer you more options for every area of the law to meet your course or on-the-job reference requirements. We now have over 140 titles from which to choose in the following areas:

Administrative Law
Alternative Dispute Resolution
Bankruptcy
Business Organizations/Corporations
Civil Litigation and Procedure
CLA Exam Preparation
Client Accounting
Computer in the Law Office
Constitutional Law
Contract Law
Criminal Law and Procedure
Document Preparation
Environmental Law
Ethics

Family Law
Federal Taxation
Intellectual Property
Introduction to Law
Introduction to Paralegalism
Law Office Management
Law Office Procedures
Legal Research, Writing, and Analysis
Legal Terminology
Paralegal Employment
Real Estate Law
Reference Materials
Torts and Personal Injury Law
Will, Trusts, and Estate Administration

You will find unparalleled, practical support

Each text is augmented by instructor and student supplements to ensure the best learning experience possible. We also offer custom publishing and other benefits such as West's Student Achievement Award. In addition, our sales representatives are ready to provide you with dependable service.

We want to hear from you

Our best contributions for improving the quality of our books and instructional materials is feedback from the people who use them. If you have a question, concern, or observation about any of our materials, or you have a product proposal or manuscript, we want to hear from you. Please contact your local representative or write us at the following address:

West Legal Studies, 3 Columbia Circle, P.O. Box 15015, Albany, NY 12212-5015

For additional information point your browser at
www.westlegalstudies.com

Legal Research
Using the Internet

JUDY A. LONG. J.D.
Paralegal Coordinator
Rio Hondo College
Whittier, CA

WEST

TM

THOMSON LEARNING

Africa • Australia • Canada • Denmark • Japan • Mexico • New Zealand • Philippines
Puerto Rico • Singapore • Spain • United Kingdom • United States

West Legal Studies:
Business Unit Director: Susan Simpfenderfer
Executive Editor: Marlene McHugh Pratt
Acquisitions Editor: Joan M. Gill
Editorial Assistant: Lisa H. Flatley
Executive Marketing Manager: Donna Lewis
Executive Production Manager: Wendy A. Troeger
Production Editor: Betty L. Dickson
Illustrator: Joseph Villanova
Cover Design: Laurie A. Boyce
Cover Image: Artville

Printed in Canada
4 5 6 7 8 9 10 XXX 05 04 03 02 01

For more information, contact Delmar, 3 Columbia Circle, PO Box 15015, Albany, NY 12212-0515; or find us on the World Wide Web at http://www.westlegalstudies.com

Library of Congress Cataloging-in-Publication Data
Long, Judy A., 1937-
    Legal research using the Internet / Judy A. Long.
       p.　cm.
    Includes bibliographical references and index.
    ISBN 0-7668-1335-5
    1. Information storage and retrieval systems—Law—United States.
  2. Legal research—United States—Computer network resources.
  3. Internet (Computer network)—United States　I. Title.
KF242.A1L66　1999   99-38664
340'.0285'4678—dc21   CIP

DEDICATION

To my husband Bill
without whose support this book would not have been completed

CONTENTS

PART II   LEGAL RESEARCH

PREFACE

For some time, books have been a lawyer's "stock in trade." Now comes the Internet! Most materials that have been available in book form are now available with a click of a mouse. A vast number of web sites are available for the legal profession as well as those individuals involved in the corporate world. The goal of this text is to present, in plain language, an introduction to what sites are available for not only lawyers but business people as well. Many of the sites presented are helpful to any lay person.

Although a considerable amount of time has been spent into doing research on the Internet to find the latest web pages, it may be possible that some of the sites have either moved or been deleted as of the printing of this book. In those cases, please e-mail me at "**Jlong@rh.cc.ca.us**" and let me know so that future editions of the book may be upgraded.

The first part of the book is devoted to conducting searches and sending e-mail. Methods of conducting general searches are presented. The latter portion of the book concentrates on the research conducted in a law office and offers alternatives to books.

The author will be teaching a class on the Internet commencing in the Fall Semester of 1999 with this book as a text. Anyone who is interested in either learning more about the course or in registering for it should go to the Rio Hondo College web page at "**http://www.rh.cc.ca.us**" and look under the "Virtual College" section. It is believed that this type of course will be extremely beneficial to those individuals who find it difficult to go to a college campus to take a class, as well as those who wish to learn how to do research on the Internet for their personal use, business use, or in law offices.

ACKNOWLEDGMENTS

Many individuals provided assistance in the preparation of this textbook. I would like to thank Joan Gill, editor, Lisa Flatley, assistant editor, and Neil Stillman, copy editor, for their help and guidance throughout the process of getting this book out as well as their assistance in securing WESTLAW access. The following individuals provided valuable suggestions and recommendations in their reviews of the text:

Laura Shiltz
  Eastern Michigan University
Jesse Frey
  CLE Online
Thomas Higgins
  Illinois Central College
Ruth Harrison
  Yavapai Community College

Of particular assistance were the many individuals on the AAfPE listserv who provided me with links to legal sites and other suggestions on teaching the course. Thanks to Julie Murthy at Virginia Intermont College, David Dye at Kapiolani College, Tom Higgins at Illinois Central College, Lenore Molee at Montclair State University, David Jordan at Los Angeles Mission College, Mary Urisko from Michigan, and Cheryl R. from New York.

A very special thanks to all of those individuals who enabled me to feature pictures of their web pages in the text, including:

Kara Thornton at West Group;
Mark Korf at West Group/West Legal Directory;
The Find Law Team at **FindLaw.com/**;
Joshua Blackman at **InternetLawyer.com**;
Robin Palmer at **Mapquest.com**;
Jan Waugh at the Association of Legal Administrators;
Rick Stroud at the International Association of Administrative
  Professionals; and
Lyn Donaldson at the National Transportation Safety Board;
Dave Haldy at **law.net**;

Juliet Smith at the WWW Virtual Library;
Martin Allen at **firstlinelaw.com**;
David W. Morris for his links to many government agencies
John Marts for his links to state and federal courts and agencies in Washington

A very special thanks to Andy Howard and Jim Hipolito from the Rio Hondo Virtual College for teaching me how to put an online course together and for their help in copying web pages.

Thanks also to anyone I may have inadvertently left off of this list.

Judy A. Long, J.D.

Please note the Internet resources are of a time sensitive nature and URL addresses may often change or be deleted.

PART
1

General

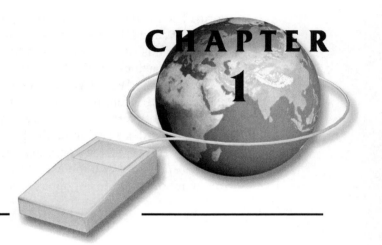

CHAPTER
1

Introduction

S ome readers may already be familiar with the Internet and the Web. This chapter is a review of Internet terminology and an introduction to the use of the Internet. An introduction to the use of the Internet requires a definition of the terms used as well as an explanation of their purposes. Being "on the Internet" is also called being in "cyberspace."

The Internet is the door to the information superhighway. Vast amounts of information are at your fingertips with the mere click of a mouse. Many computers join together to comprise the Internet, which then provides the means for many computers to share information and communicate with each other. Computers all over the world are connected to the Internet via the World Wide Web, or simply, the "Web." Sometimes you will hear these terms used interchangeably. The World Wide Web is commonly referred to also by its abbreviation, "WWW."

TERMINOLOGY

The **Internet** is a network composed of thousands of computer networks—the largest ever created. **Networks** are made up of many computers linked together, either locally within an organization (a **LAN** or **local area network**), or more widely over a larger geographic area (a **WAN** or **wide area network**.) Picture a large law office with branches all over the world. The local branch of the office would have its computers connected via a **LAN,** and all of its offices would be connected via a **WAN.** Now picture thousands of LANs and WANs all over the world and you have an idea of the vastness of the Internet.

Although the **World Wide Web** (or Web) provides a means to connect the various different parts of the Internet, and as mentioned above some people use both terms interchangeably, the two are not identical. The Web actually provides a search method for finding information on the Internet using **hypertext,** which combines pictures and text that connect to other pictures and text. With the use of the Web, one is able to obtain information in not only text form, but as video, graphics, sound, and animation as well.

CONNECTING TO THE INTERNET

In order to connect to the Internet, you will need a modem with your computer as well as a subscription to an **Internet service provider ("ISP").** If you are connecting from your school, the computer you are using must have "Internet access"; that is, the ability to connect to the Internet. If you are using this text as part of a course on the Internet, then you will already have a computer with Internet access or an account for the use of your school's computers.

A **modem** allows computers to talk to each other via telephone lines. If your computer has a modem, it will also have a plug and cord that must be plugged into your computer as well as a telephone wall jack. If you have one telephone line, then when you are using the modem no telephone calls may be made or received. Many people who use the Internet a great deal have two lines, one for their telephone and one for their modem. In this way, you may still receive and make telephone calls while you are using the modem. However, you will then have a double telephone bill.

There are many providers of Internet access. Investigate different companies. Talk to your friends who use the Internet to determine which providers they use, and if they are happy with their services. Some providers have frequent disconnects, which can be frustrating when you are in the middle of a research project and are suddenly disconnected from the line. If you are connected from work or school, this decision will have been made by the individuals in charge at that location. However, it is usually recommended that you have access from your home computer as well.

NAMES AND ADDRESSES ON THE INTERNET————————

At your office or school, you may have a name and address already assigned. For instance, at the school where the author teaches, all employees use their first initial and last name for a name and the school's Internet address for an address. Thus, my address becomes:

JLong@rh.cc.ca.us

Use an "@" sign to separate the person's name and the address.

If you have Internet access at home, you will have to choose a name and the provider will generally have its own address. For instance, if you are using America Online, your address will end with:

_____@aol.com

Many Internet experts advise individuals not to use their first names in their Internet addresses. Therefore, a typical name using the above address might be JLong; the name and address then becomes:

JLong@aol.com

This is the name and address anyone should use when sending you e-mail, discussed below.

E-MAIL————————————————————————————

Sending correspondence via the Internet is practically instantaneous. You may write to someone in another part of the country or world, or perhaps across town, and she will receive the mail within minutes of the time you sent it. Internet providers have forms to use to send e-mail. In the name portion, use the name as discussed above with the appropriate address, similar to the manner in which you send regular mail (known as "snail mail" on the Internet.) If you dislike typing, software programs are available that will allow you to talk into a microphone and have the computer do the typing for you, programs similar to using dictating equipment.

Internet names may also give you information about the location of the individual. The following sites or locations are indicated by the extensions in their names:

.com	commercial site (often used by private ISPs)
.gov	a government site
.mil	a military site
.org	an organization
.edu	education
.ca	California or Canada
.uk	United Kingdom

NAMES FORMAT

Most Internet addresses are comprised of capital and lower case letters. All lower case letters usually function in any case. No spaces should be placed in an Internet name. When giving your name to someone, spell out each portion of the name unless the spelling is obvious. "@" should be given as "at."

WEB PAGE ADDRESSES

In addition to the names used for e-mail, other names are used to reach various web pages. These addresses are known as location numbers or URLs (Uniform Resource Locator). In order to access a page on the Internet, URL must be used. If you wished to access the web page for West Publishing Company, you would type the following address in the "Go to" section of your Internet provider after you have accessed your account:

http://www.westgroup.com

This address is the URL for West Publishing Company. Most large corporations have their own web pages, which are accessed via their web address (or URL.)

Note that Internet addresses generally begin with "http://www." and in many cases are followed by an abbreviation of the company's name you are accessing. For instance, the web site for Northwest Airlines is "http://www.nwa.com". When you key in the address at the "go to" portion of your screen, you will be taken to the web page for Northwest Airlines. This information is useful if you are doing a search to find a particular organization and are not able to find it. Sometimes just abbreviating the name and using ".com" will take you to a company site.

SEARCHES

Several search tools are available for you to find information on the Internet. Your ISP will usually have its own search engine, or you may prefer to use others as well. Some of the more common are menu driven. That is, they provide a list of categories in which you can search. Examples are GOPHER and VERONICA.

Others provide a key word search that enables you to list all key words in which you are interested. An example is AOLNET. The computer will search the Internet and provide you with an abstract of all documents that have your key words within them. They are listed by percentage of key word occurrence, with the highest numbers first.

Suppose you want articles that give you information on California cases involving palimony. You would type the following words into the search box:

California palimony cases

If you want the exact wording to appear in the documents, then type the key words in quotes as follows:

"California palimony cases"

This type search is similar to those with which some of you may be familiar from using WESTLAW. Sometimes the key words will have to be changed or modified to yield more specific search results. At other times the key words you choose may be too specific and may have to be made more general. Be prepared for a lengthy search no matter what the subject is, though, as there is a vast amount of information out there on the Internet.

Many web pages display "hyperlinks" that will connect you to other pages. These take the form of colored and/or underlined titles. You can click your mouse on the title and be taken directly to the web page referred to by the hyperlink. Documents are linked to each other over the Web, allowing you to move from one to the other by clicking on the highlighted text.

Figure 1-1 shows a typical search page on the Internet with keywords listed.

Yahoo

This site represents one of the most extensive collection of links to web sites on the Internet. It contains a tremendous collection of links to law

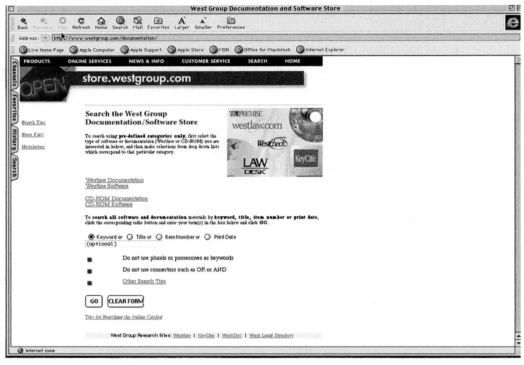

FIGURE 1-1   Key Word Search page

firms with web pages. Approximately 30,000 web locations may be found by a search on Yahoo, which may be found at:

http://dir.yahoo.com/government/law/

Some Internet providers allow access to Yahoo by merely keying "Yahoo" in the "Go to" category.

Internet Card Catalog

This site works much as a standard library card catalog. It is an excellent subject matter index for most sources available on the Internet. For general research purposes, this may be the best starting point available. It may be accessed at:

http://www.andsoforth.com

HYPERTEXT LINKS

Sometimes when you are reading information on a web page, you will notice text that is underlined or shown in a different color. This text represents a hypertext link, called a "hyperlink," to another web page. If you click your mouse on that word or group of words, it will take you immediately to another area of the Web. In some cases, you will find web pages with lists of hypertext links in a given subject area. For instance, some colleges provide hyperlinks on their web pages to different areas of the college or research materials about given topics.

For example, suppose you were on the web page for the Codes of California. Listed there will be the various codes, all names underlined as hypertext links. If you click on the *Penal Code,* you will be immediately taken to the Penal Code of California. Once you find a page you wish to refer to in the future, you may bookmark that page to enable you to have immediate access to it. Some software applications refer to this bookmark as "favorite places." With a page bookmarked, you can click on its title from the bookmark list and immediately go to that page without taking the time to do a search or key in its address.

GRAPHICS IN BROWSERS

GUIs (Graphical User Interfaces) are used in browser programs such as Netscape, Internet Explorer, and Mosaic and are icons or graphics on web pages that enable you to execute commands on your computer. For example, icons may be available for stopping, going back to the previous page, going to the home page, scrolling, or going forward. Some of the commands on these pages are similar to those used in Windows. See Figure 1-2 for a sample web page with a GUI.

GETTING STARTED

In the previous sections, basic descriptions were provided of the terminology used on the Internet, and fundamental explanations given for gaining access to and using it. Now we will get started on actually going online and finding some material. Fasten your seat belt, as you are about to undertake an exciting journey on the information superhighway.

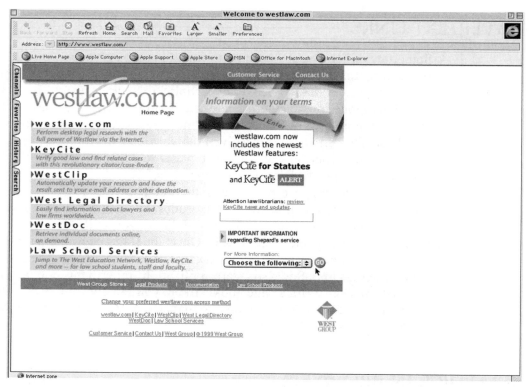

FIGURE 1-2   Graphical user interface Netscape Web page

1. **Open your browser**   Be sure your computer is turned on and look for the icon that shows your particular browser. Double click the icon with your mouse. Depending on where you are signing on from, you will probably need a user name and password to get "online." Additionally, your school may have a web page that loads first when the browser opens, and acts as the "home page" when you first go online from your college. Generally, the browser takes a few minutes to load, so be patient. When the hourglass shows on the computer screen, your browser is loading. It is fully loaded when the hourglass turns into an arrow.

   Think of the home page as your home on the Internet. From your "home" you may visit many other sites, but returning home just takes a click on the "home" icon.

2. **Find other sites**   Scroll down your home page to become familiar with its contents. If you see an item of interest, and it is underlined or in color, click on this hyperlink to be taken to its site. You may continue to click on hyperlinks on subsequent pages several·times and may even find yourself in another part of the world. Now look at your watch to see the amount of time that has elapsed. Time passes quickly on the Internet.

3. **Go back home**   Returning to your home page may be done quickly or with detours along the way. Suppose you want to return to your home page immediately. Click on the "Home" icon and you are home again.

   But what if you previously found an interesting site and forgot how to get to it. Just hit the "back" button and it will move you backwards to the other sites you have been on. Click "home" to go home by driving forward and directly; click "back" to go home by driving backwards with stops along the way.

   Another method for retracing your steps is by using the "View History" command from the pull-down menu. The names of all previously visited pages since leaving "home" will appear. Click on the one that you want to return to visit.

See Figures 1-3A and 1-3B for examples of home pages with pull-down menus for viewing the history folder.

DISPLAYING ADDRESS OF CURRENT LOCATION

Browsers usually display the address of the present location in a box at the top of the screen. In many cases, showing the location is a default setting; however, in those cases where the default has to be set, follow these steps:

1. Select "Show Location" or "Show Current URL" from the Options pull down menu.
2. Follow the instructions for turning that option on.
3. Check the address portion at the top of the page to be sure the current address is displayed.
4. If possible, change the Options to reflect this as the default option.

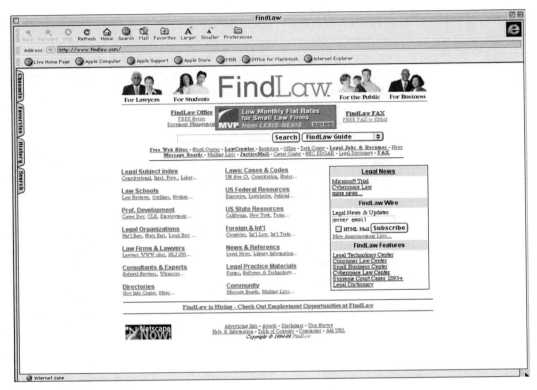

FIGURE 1-3A   FindLaw Home page

INFORMATION ABOUT THE INTERNET

The best information about the Internet may be found on the Internet itself. Do a key word search using the word "Internet" and many items will be displayed. Click on those that actually give you information about the Internet itself. Check the date on the home page to determine the last date it was updated. Most home pages will display this date. If the update was recent, then the home page information is probably up-to-date.

But suppose the page was not updated in the last year. That means that all information on the page was current as of a year ago. With the vast number of changes occurring every day on the Internet, you would not want to use this page for current information.

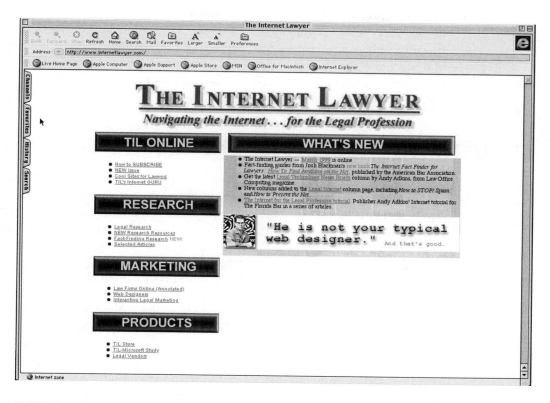

FIGURE 1-3B   Internet Lawyer page

OBSOLETE URLs

Sometimes you will click into a page from your Bookmarks and find that the page no longer exists. In that case, you may have to do a new search for its location. Many pages change locations often, and the page you found three months ago may not be there today. Sometimes the new page address is given on the old page; other times you may have to do a completely new search to find it. In this case, be sure to delete the obsolete page from your bookmarks and add the new page name.

TIMING OUT

Some Internet pages are very popular and are difficult to access because of the number of individuals attempting to load them at the same time. In those cases, you may get a "timed out" message when attempting to reach the site. This is similar to a busy signal on a telephone. Keep trying until you reach the site. In some cases, if a page is taking a long time to load, it helps to hit "stop" and "reload" to reload the page more quickly.

ETIQUETTE ON THE INTERNET ("NETIQUETTE")——————

Just as in everyday life, there are certain things that you should do and others that you should not do on the Internet. The key is to remember to be polite, whether it be in an e-mail message, a bulletin board posting, or a chat room meeting. Remember that the other individuals with whom you are communicating cannot see your facial expressions and do not know whether you are smiling or frowning.

Some individuals who subscribe to newsgroups intentionally try to offend others and are entertained when another person becomes offended. These people post to newsgroups and oppose the consensus views of the group in a derogatory fashion. For example, one may post to a newsgroup whose topic is golf and write "Golf is a dumb game. How could anyone chase a little ball around a golf course?" Of course, the golfers who post regularly to the group are offended and wish to respond. This person welcomes the responses and is happy to rile the group. The common Internet name for this type of individual is a "SNERT". He/She is looking for a reaction and his/her messages are known as "flame-bait."

A common term used in these situations is "flame," which means a communication that vehemently disapproves of someone else's posting. It is much better to be polite in your postings rather than to flame or be "flamed." If you are the source of offense to someone, even if innocently, it is best to apologize. Also, beware of using all capital letters in your postings; this is known as "shouting" on the Internet. It may be used occasionally for emphasis but is usually frowned upon.

When responding to a message, it may be appropriate to quote part of the previous message, but never copy the whole message. Make your messages brief and to the point. Separate paragraphs with one blank line, just as you do in regular correspondence. Do not make your e-mails all one paragraph when covering several topics.

Proofread your messages to be certain that their spelling and sentence structure are correct, and then a second time to be sure they will not offend the recipient. If you are attempting to inject humor into the message, then use the "emoticon" for a happy face:

:))) or :-)))

SUMMARY

In this chapter, you have learned the basics of accessing the Internet, and how to do a simple search using key words and other methods.

Different search methods were described; examples of problems that may be encountered were discussed; and new vocabulary terms were defined.

⊕ EXERCISES

1. Locate the web page of a major airline that flies from a city close to your location to New York City. Find the fares for a flight leaving 14 days from today in the early morning hours. Assume this will be a round-trip flight. Put the URL address of the airline in the space below and the fares and information about the flight date, time, and flight number. Be sure *not* to actually make a reservation on the flight but merely make an inquiry.

   Address: **http://www.** _____

   Flight Information: _____

2. Suppose you would like to take a class at your college through the Internet. Find classes that you need to graduate in your major (including general education classes) that are offered through the Virtual College on the Internet at the college that you attend. How many units

   can you take by this method? _____

3. Is it possible to register on the Internet for classes at your college? _____

4. List five items of interest that are included in your college's home page.

   1. _____

   2. _____

   3. _____

   4. _____

   5. _____

CHAPTER 2

How to Use the Internet

INTRODUCTION

In the first chapter, we reviewed some of the key terms used on the Internet. You learned how to gain access to the Internet and find materials by doing key-word searches. In this chapter, we will explore the various tools available on the Internet and how to use them. We will discuss methods of communication, how to arrange travel, find individuals or businesses, and learn about traffic in your city.

E-MAIL: USES, ADVANTAGES, AND DISADVANTAGES

Even those individuals who do not do research on the Internet will use electronic mail, commonly known as e-mail. E-mail is a fast method of Internet communication by which the recipient receives your messages almost immediately after you send them. They may respond in the same fashion. The only necessary component to e-mail use is that both parties have an Internet address.

In today's business world, most offices are connected via e-mail. If the business has a LAN or a WAN, a connection to the Internet, or an online service, it will have e-mail capability. You may have noticed that most business cards now display e-mail address as well as telephone and fax numbers. How much more convenient it is to send someone an e-mail rather than play "telephone tag" for several days! You may also send the same e-mail to several people at the same time, which adds to its efficiency. The Internet's greatest single activity is e-mail.

Imagine the tons of paper that are saved by the use of e-mail instead of standard "snail mail" sent through the postal service. From an environmental standpoint, envision how many trees are saved by e-mail.

E-mail has all of the advantages and none of the disadvantages of postal mail and telephone calls. It eliminates "phone tag" because it does not matter if the recipient is at home when the e-mail is sent. It is also less expensive than any other means of communication since it is virtually free, except for the cost of the ISP and telephone line. If you have local access in the city where you live, then the telephone charges are nominal. Most ISPs have local access numbers through which to connect to the Internet, so that e-mail may be sent over a local line. A local telephone call is almost always charged as part of a low flat monthly rate, or at a minor charge per phone call (10¢–15¢); in both cases connection time is unlimited and no further charges are incurred. This holds true for anyone in the country, and also the world, who has an e-mail address. You can send an e-mail message to a friend in London, for example, as long as she has an e-mail address, at little cost.

Each individual with e-mail has a unique mailing address. No two people may have the same address. In order to send an e-mail, you must know the person's exact address or your mail will either go to the wrong person or be returned to you marked "address unknown." Many ISPs have an address book set up for you so that you can store other people's e-mail addresses in your own database. Many companies and schools have an on-line directory set up as an address book for you within your e-mail system.

But suppose you would like to have free e-mail; you do not necessarily need Internet service. Some of the larger, well-established companies providing this service include the following:

1. Hotmail—**http://www.hotmail.com**
2. iName—**http://www.iname.com**
3. NetAddress—**http://www.netaddress.com**

Free e-mail is also provided through major directory sites such as the following, if you have an ISP:

1. Yahoo—**http://www.yahoo.com**
2. AltaVista—**http://www.altavista.com**
3. Excite—**http://www.excite.com**

One disadvantage of these free e-mail systems is that usually e-mail cannot be composed offline at your own pace, a service which is available through some ISPs, if you have the required software installed on your hard drive.

However, the major advantage of these systems is that one may send and receive messages from any computer with an Internet connection and a browser. Travelers may thus access e-mail from business centers, other offices, airline clubs, cyber cafes, and hotel computer kiosks, without the necessity of carrying a laptop and dealing with special plugs and adapters, often required in foreign countries, and without the fear of the laptop being lost or stolen.

America Online enables its users to access their e-mail from another computer by using the Web at:

http://www.aol.com/netmail/home.html

PARTS OF THE E-MAIL

1. **Caption or heading**   The caption of your e-mail message resembles that of an interoffice memorandum. It contains the following items:

   TO:
   SUBJECT:

   The date you send the e-mail will appear automatically, as will your name. Often the time appears as well.

   Be sure to key in the individual's exact Internet address, along with the proper subject. In many cases, the ISP automatically places your e-mail address in the "FROM:" portion of the e-mail form. If the recipient may not know the designation is your address, you may wish to put your name in the "SUBJECT:" portion of the form. For instance, suppose your e-mail address is **Jdoe@aol.com** and the recipient is not familiar with your last name. In the subject portion, you may put "From Jane Doe regarding Internet Meeting."

2. **Copies**   If you would like to send a copy of the e-mail to another individual, then key in his e-mail address here, in the "cc:" portion of the form. If you would like to send a blind copy (one that the

other recipients do not know is being sent), then put the person's address in parentheses as follows:

(Jdoe@aol.com)

Only Jdoe and you will know that he received a copy of the message.

3. **Body**   In the "message" portion of the e-mail, it is not always necessary to use the same formal language often used in a letter. You should prepare the e-mail in block style, using a clear and concise writing style. If you want an answer within a certain time period, indicate the due date in the last paragraph of the e-mail, just as you would do in a letter. Although it is usually not possible to sign the e-mail, a closing with your name should be included.

    A more informal style may be used when writing to friends.

    E-mail may be signed if the writer uses a scanner to scan in a signature. Copy or multimedia centers provide this service for a fee.

4. **Attachments**   In some cases you may wish to attach other material to the e-mail. As long as you have this material on your computer in another file, you may do so. In order to send an attachment, you must key in the name of the document in the attachment portion, or "browse" for it using this function of your e-mail software. Some applications enable you to search your files and drag the attachment into the body of the e-mail.

    You may attach documents, pictures, graphics, or any other item that you have on your computer's hard drive. You may wish to scan pictures and send them to a relative via e-mail. You may scan exhibits for a lawsuit and send them attached to an e-mail. You may wish to send a draft of a pleading or document for review by a colleague.

HOW SECURE IS THE INTERNET?

Much has been written about security problems on the Internet. How can you be assured that when you send an e-mail it will be received and read by only the recipient? What about those times when one person gets the e-mail for a large department and distributes it in printed form? Are there hackers out there who can obtain anyone's e-mail? Unfortunately, there *are* serious security problems in the use of the Internet. Service providers have the capability to access subscribers' e-mail. The same is true for system administrators for large organizations. However, it can be said that the Internet is just as secure as most other communications devices.

With the widespread use of cordless and cellular telephones, individual conversations are readily available to anyone with the proper interception equipment. Scramblers are available for most devices, but both parties must have the same type of scrambler for the message to be received and transmitted properly. The same is true for the Internet. There are devices on the market to encode e-mail, but the sender needs an encoder device and the receiver needs a decoder device.

An equally prevalent problem is sending e-mail to the wrong person. Most Internet providers enable you to have your own address book of e-mail addresses for people to whom you frequently send e-mail. The list is accessible by a click of the mouse; the address is put into the e-mail with a click of the mouse; the e-mail is sent with a click of the mouse. In three clicks you can access the address book and send an e-mail out. Suppose in your haste you click on the wrong address. Instantly that e-mail is sent to the wrong person.

Or imagine the scenario of keying in someone's name and e-mail address. One typographical error might send that e-mail to the wrong person. Anyone with an e-mail account knows how easy it is to receive an e-mail intended for someone else.

It is advisable to not send confidential communications via e-mail. Sometimes it is beneficial if the sender and recipient have their own coding system in which certain words mean certain other words.

PASSWORD SECURITY

Many people think their accounts and communications are secure because their Internet account requires a password to "log on". This may be the case if an uncommon password is used. However, most people use common words, names, or numbers. Password thieves know the most common names to use to try to access another's account. Try to make your password something only you know. Do not use your social security number, address, age, or date of birth; do not use any family names. Memorize your password and do not write it down where anyone else might find it.

It has been said that anyone going through an office complex late at night would be able to find a majority of passwords by just looking at people's computers. Some individuals use a post-it note attached to their computer screen with their passwords written on it. Any note found with a one-word name written on it is likely a password.

ORGANIZING YOUR E-MAIL

Most e-mail software furnishes features that allow you to organize your e-mail into "In Boxes," "Out Boxes," "New Mail," " Sent Items," and other folders. Purge your "In Box" and "Sent Items" often and carefully, first determine whether it is necessary to actually save each message contained in these folders. Your "In Box" will include all mail that has been sent to you and read by you; the "Out Box" will include all mail you have composed but not yet sent; the "New Mail Box" will contain mail you have not yet read; and the "Sent Items" folder will include those e-mails you have sent out. Some ISPs allow you additional e-mail address designations (the part of the e-mail address preceding the "@" symbol; the part following it remains the same for any given provider).

Some Internet providers will only save your e-mail for a certain period of time to avoid taking up space on their system, or "services," so it may become necessary to make copies of e-mail that you wish to save permanently. In some cases, you may be able to save it to your hard drive under another document name.

SENDING YOUR E-MAIL

The best way to learn how to send e-mail is to actually do it. Open your e-mail program and we will go through the steps together. Let us begin by sending ourselves an e-mail message. Often the author sends herself messages from home to her office or office to home.

Key your e-mail address into the "To" section. Make your subject "Test" and type "test" in the message. Then click the "SEND" button; which is usually located to the right of the e-mail message as you face the screen. Instantly this message will be sent to you. Open the message, close it, and delete it. You may delete it by highlighting the message in the list of received messages. Be sure to close the message before highlighting it. Hit the "delete" key and the message will be deleted.

If you wish to delete several messages at the same time, highlight the first message you wish to delete. Holding down the "alt" and "shift" keys on the lower left of your keyboard, highlight the last message you wish to delete. Hit the "delete" key and all of those messages will be deleted.

ADDRESS BOOKS

Your e-mail software may furnish a place to put frequently used e-mail addresses, called an "address book." It would have a place for the person or business name, designation, and e-mail address. To use the address book, open the "compose mail" or "write mail" icon and another icon will appear on the e-mail form called "Address Book." Click on the address book and a list of names will appear. Click on the name of the desired recipient of your e-mail and it will appear in the "TO" portion of the e-mail. Different service providers have variations of this system.

CONDUCTING A SEARCH

Depending on the ISP utilized, various search engines are available on its home page to search the Internet for a given topic. For example, suppose you want to find airline web pages. You would go to the search engine on the ISPs home page and use the key word "airlines" for your search. If this returns too long a list of resultant web pages, then you may wish to narrow your key words to produce a more specific and shorter list of pages. The search engine will list web pages that have your key words appearing in their text, along with a brief description of each page. If you wish a certain set of words to appear in all responses, then your key words should be quoted, such as "American Airlines." In this case, only those pages with the exact phrase "American Airlines" will show. Generally the pages are listed in the order in which the largest number of key words appear with greatest frequency.

Various private web pages exist for the purpose of providing search capabilities on many topics. One particularly comprehensive page that is very effective for doing general research is located at:

http://www.refdesk.com/

FINDING A PERSON OR BUSINESS ONLINE

Many ISPs provide their own "white pages" to find people and "yellow pages" to find businesses. Searches may be conducted by name or geographical location. Suppose you have a friend in another state but do not know your friend's address (physical, not e-mail address). You could search by your friend's name and the state to determine her/his address and, in many cases, telephone number. Note that some individuals and businesses may not be included in these directories.

Several directories of lawyers exist online and will be discussed in the Legal Research section below.

If you are looking for a telephone number, area code, or e-mail address, several web databases are searched simultaneously by using this site:

http://www.555-1212.com

Yellow pages also exist for finding telephone numbers and addresses of businesses. Door-to-door driving directions may be obtained as well at:

http://www.zip2.com

Web pages exist for investigation firms that will search many databases, for a fee, to find people. One such site is located at:

http://www.ameri.com/sherlock/sherlock.htm

A good starting point for locating businesses, people, telephone numbers, e-mail addresses and to obtain maps is available at a site called "The Ultimates," located at

http://www.theultimates.com

A large number of links to other web sites are available at this site for searching white pages, yellow pages, e-mail addresses, and mapping services. Reverse residential telephone number searches may be performed as well. It is even possible to obtain the names of everyone who live on a particular street along with their addresses and telephone numbers. If time is of the essence it may be better to hire an investigation firm rather than try to conduct the search yourself.

The Social Security Administration provides a web page to search over 60 million names to find death information. If you know the person's name, and/or location, or social security number, a search may be conducted to determine the person's date of death and last known address. If you have only the person's name, all individuals with that name will be listed.

MEETINGS ONLINE

Most of the publicity heard about "chat rooms" indicates that they are places where dangerous things can happen because people often use other names and can remain relatively anonymous. However, the "chat room" may be used effectively for private meetings of businesses or law firms. Providers that have "chat" capability also give the subscriber the ability to set up a "private" chat room and invite only specific individuals.

A marketing consultant in Canada may speak online to a client in New York without incurring long distance telephone charges by setting up a chat room for this purpose. A lawyer in Washington may set up a meeting in a chat room with members of the same firm located in New York. A judge at the World Court in New York may set up a room to meet with opposing lawyers from Japan and Russia in a lawsuit to discuss fishing rights. Staff meetings may be conducted with branch offices in other parts of the country or other countries as well. Endless possibilities exist for the constructive use of chat rooms to conduct business.

TRAVEL

Even with the use of chat rooms, it often becomes necessary to travel to other cities and countries. A considerable amount of information is available on the Internet for this purpose, including weather, hotels, cities, and maps, as well as travel reservations capability.

Many travel agencies specialize in online reservations. Most airlines also have their own web sites where reservations may be made.

One interesting site that provides a considerable amount of travel information is located at:

http://www.thetrip.com

This site enables you to make plane reservations, and provides guides and travel news for successful trips to many different areas. It also has the ability to track a flight in progress once it leaves its origination point. A new feature of this site is that it will notify up to three people by e-mail when a flight arrives at its destination. This may prove valuable in cases where people are arriving from different cities to attend a meeting.

Other sites that provide travel information and reservations include the following:

http://www.frommers.com

Travel information is provided by Arthur Frommer. The site is known as his Encyclopedia of Travel.

http://www.biztravel.com

This site specializes in business travel but also provides information for the leisure traveler. One may make flight, hotel and car reservations, track frequent-flyer miles, and learn about special fares.

http://www.itn.com

The Internet Travel Network monitors the lowest fares between cities and provides flight reservations.

http://www.travelocity.com

Preview Travel provides a means for making flight, hotel, and automobile reservations, and reports on special fares when available. Their Farefinder search engine searches airline databases to find the lowest fares between major United States cities.

In order to assist travelers who prefer to stay at hotels that have an in-room computer with Internet access, *Forbes* magazine has developed "Rooms with a Clue" at:

http://www.forbes.com

The site provides rate and contact information, and displays the hotel's telephone jack type, power plug type, and whether the telephone system is digital or analog.

Travel Abroad

Information about obtaining passports is available on the State Department's home page at:

http://www.state.gov/index.html

The State Department provides a page where individuals may check to determine what countries had travel warnings issued concerning them. These warnings are issued when the State Department decides to recommend that Americans avoid travel to a particular country. Public announcements disseminate information about terrorist threats and other conditions posing significant risks to the security of American travelers. Such warnings are issued when there is a perceived threat that will include Americans as a particular target group. Some examples of these announcements include short-term coups, bomb threats to airlines, violence by terrorists and anniversary dates of specific terrorist events. This information is available at:

http://www.travel.state.gov/warnings_list.html

General information about Europe's large cities may be found in a virtual tour of its countries. The site includes films, photographs, audio, and virtual reality experiences. The site is available at:

http://www.1-call.co.uk/webcentral/europe.html

To find a multimedia unit on Italy with 360-degree virtual reality, see:

http://www.wandering.com

Local Travel

Sometimes it becomes necessary to travel across town to a new location. Some sources for maps and directions from one address to another are:

http://www.mapquest.com

http://www.mapblast.com

http://www.mapsonus.com

These sites provide directions and maps to all parts of the country. Figure 2-1 displays the main Mapquest search page.

Some traffic information is available on the Internet for various large cities and metropolitan areas. The appropriate web site for this purpose is:

http://smartraveler.com

This site was begun by the Department of Transportation in California. However, it has been expanded to include information for other large metropolitan areas. Traffic information for California is particularly valuable as it gives complete freeway statistics and is usually updated at 15-minute intervals. Often alternate routes may be planned when the freeway is backed up at any given spot.

A map of the United States highlighting the following large metropolitan areas is a recent addition to the site:

Los Angeles

San Francisco

San Diego

Seattle

Denver

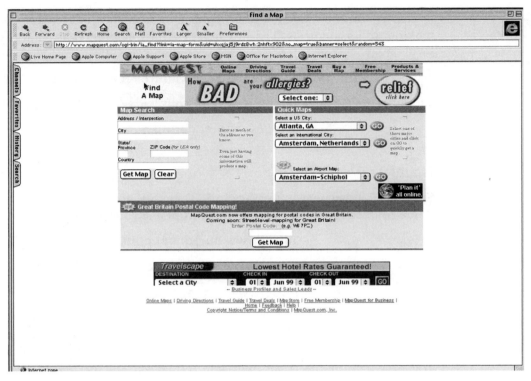

FIGURE 2-1 Mapquest web page: Find A Map

Dallas

Houston

Minneapolis/St. Paul

Chicago

Detroit

Boston

New York

Philadelphia

Washington, D.C.

If you click on the name of the city, you will be taken to that city's perti-nent traffic information: the maps of the different highways, freeways, and interstates; with traffic speeds at given points of different routes; and information on incidents, construction closures, and weather. Some city maps provide information for major highways only. The Los Angeles section is particularly comprehensive and shows the information for all freeways in the southern California area.

LISTSERVS

A listserv can be considered a subscription to e-mail on a given topic. Once you register for the listserv, all mail sent out to the listserv is also sent to you. It is a free service that may prove valuable for individuals interested in various topics. For example, the author subscribes to a listserv of paralegal educators and receives daily communications about information of interest in that area.

There are two different types of listservs, one which enables everyone on the list to post messages (discussion lists), and one which only allows certain individuals to post (distribution list). In order to subscribe to a listserv, you must use the address for the listserv. Once you have subscribed to the listserv, you may use the address for the discussion group in order to post to the group. Or you can key a response to an e-mail that has been sent by the listserv to you and hit "reply to all."

Once you have subscribed to a listserv, you will receive a confirmation back via e-mail almost immediately. Usually you will be required to send back a confirmation that you in fact have subscribed to the listserv. The next e-mail you receive from the listserv will list detailed instructions on the protocol for the group. It is a good idea to print this message, so that you know the proper procedures for this particular group.

The best way to find a listserv of interest is by word of mouth. Books are also available with names of listservs. Once you subscribe to one listserv, you will often receive information about others as well. Suppose, however, that after subscribing to one listserv, you are interested in finding out what others are available on that topic. You may send an e-mail to the listserv address with the following information in the body:

LISTS GLOBAL/law

LISTS GLOBAL/education

or any other topic in which you are interested after the "/" symbol.

NEWSGROUPS (USENET)

Newsgroups provide an international bulletin board with thousands of topics and hundreds of thousands of different conversations. There are newsgroups on every topic imaginable, from academic discussions to sporting events. Within newsgroups you can find images, sounds, and software that you can download to your computer. Newsgroups constitute the second widest usage of the Internet, after e-mail.

A newsreader program is required for anyone who wishes to participate in a newsgroup. This allows you to subscribe to newsgroups, so that you can read newsgroup articles as well as post messages. Major categories include computers, news, recreation, sports, and various special, regional, or local groups. Often a group will be created that relates to a current event that is presently in high profile in the news, such as the Y2K problem.

Newsgroups allow an individual to post notices, send or distribute notices to the group, and publish discussion items. You may think of newsgroups as giant bulletin boards or discussion groups.

SUMMARY

In this chapter we discussed many standard uses of the Internet that are not specifically law related. The most critical area is the use of e-mail, which can instantly connect us to anyone else in the world who might have an e-mail address. It enables you to correspond with anyone having an e-mail address, and receive a response as soon as the recipient reads your message and writes back.

Many sorts of travel arrangements are possible on the Internet. Plane, hotel, and automobile reservations may be made on the Internet. Weather may be found for other parts of the country and the world. Maps may be prepared covering unfamiliar street addresses, cities, and even states. Traffic patterns may be found for many different cities.

Meetings may be conducted online by using private chat rooms. These chat rooms may connect businesses in other parts of the country and the world.

⊕ EXERCISES

1. Prepare an e-mail to your instructor telling her what you learned in this chapter.

2. Search the Internet to find a Newsgroup in which you are interested.
   What is its address?   Http://www. _____
   What is the subject of the newsgroup? _____

3. Make a map from your home to your school. What is the mileage?

   _____

   What is the estimated time it takes to go between the two points?

   _____

4. Access a newsgroup that is of interest to you. Post a notice on it and hand in a copy.

5. Explain the differences among e-mail, listservs, and newsgroups.

6. List the best web sites to use if traveling to Europe and what each site provides.

Legal Research

CHAPTER 3

General Information

In the last two chapters you learned how to conduct research on the Internet and the World Wide Web. A law office requires a considerable amount of this research. For example, lawyers, paralegals, and other law office personnel send e-mail to the firm, other offices, and to other locations. They travel to other parts of the country and world on business trips.

Finding adverse parties in lawsuits may be done via the various search engines available on the Internet, as discussed in Chapter 2. Now we will discuss the specialized search mechanisms available for the legal profession, along with the sites you would utilize for your legal research.

SEARCHES

The Library of Congress maintains a web page that provides a catalog of all available publications. You can search for any book that has been published and has an ISBN number. Searches may be undertaken by title, key words, or author. The site for the Library of Congress is located at:

http://lcweb.loc.gov/

One of the more comprehensive web pages for finding information about different areas of law is available at:

http://www.amicus.ca/legallinks

This site provides information on specific practice areas along with background information on law-related topics. It is particularly useful for finding resources in a practice area with which you are unfamiliar or where more information is required than can be found under the federal or state links. The site includes the following practice areas of law:

1. Bankruptcy
2. Business law
3. Civil litigation
4. Commercial law
5. Constitutional law and civil rights
6. Corporate safety
7. Criminal law
8. Employment law
9. Family law
10. Health and disability law
11. Insurance law
12. Labor law
13. Environmental law
14. Probate law
15. Real property law
16. Personal injury

Resources are available on the growing body of law governing Internet use, as well as additional links connected to this subject. General links are provided to hardware and software information along with leads to doing searches.

LINKS TO LAW SITES

FindLaw has been touted as being the best site to find other legal resources. Their web page is available at:

http://www.findlaw.com/

Some of the links available on the FindLaw site include information for the following:

1. Consumer law
2. United States Supreme Court cases
3. State cases and laws
4. Law schools
5. Legal subject indexes
6. State law resources
7. Foreign and international resources
8. Law firms
9. Legal organizations
10. Government directories
11. Legal practice materials

If you are looking for a site on a law subject and do not know the web site address, it is often easier to find the site on FindLaw than to do a search on your own. It is especially valuable if you are not sure exactly what topic under which to conduct your key word search. Figure 3-1 displays the main FindLaw web site.

One site that provides links to legal information may be found at:

http://www.law.indiana.edu/v-lib

The latter is called the World Wide Web Virtual Law Library and is arranged by subject. It includes links to sites of specialty areas of law, law firms, government resources, law journals, and search engines.

One site that provides three categories of information is located at:

http://law.net/roundnet.html

Links are available to legal resources, legal services, and attorneys by practice areas.

A comparable guide may be found at Cornell's Legal Information Institute at:

http://www.law.cornell.edu/index.html

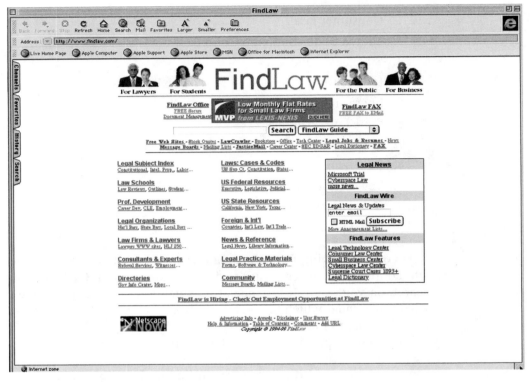

FIGURE 3-1   Main FindLaw web site

Lawstreet's site provides links to many specialty practice areas, as well as links to international law, federal and state law. This site provides a searchable database and is located at:

http://www.lawstreet.com/LawGuide/index.cfm

The American Bar Association maintains a Legal Research Law Link that has links to all branches of government as well as the courts, Judicial Council, court home pages, law school libraries, and a number of other legal reference resources. It is located at:

http://www.abanet.org

A large online catalog containing records for over 10 million holdings in libraries throughout the University of California system is its MELVYL home page, located at:

http://www.melvyl.ucop.edu/

LEGAL DOCUMENTS

Customized legal documents are provided at:

http://www.legaldocs.com/

This web page enables the user to prepare customized documents online from given templates. Some of these documents are free, and others require a small payment. Documents are available in the areas of wills, trusts, sales, leases, partnerships, employment, business, and real estate. Simple wills are available free of charge and may be prepared by completing a questionnaire that is provided on the web page. Remember that these documents are generic in nature; therefore, state laws should always be reviewed for the state in which the document is being prepared and filed to ascertain whether that document is valid in that particular state.

LAW OFFICE TECHNOLOGY

A site that includes articles on technology and its legal effects is located at:

http://www.nettechinc.com/default.asp

KEY WORD SEARCHES

Searching by key word for legal resources is similar to general searches. Those who have used WESTLAW or LEXIS are already familiar with key word searches.

Try to think of all words that describe the material for which you are searching. Using a general term when you are looking for specific information yields too large a result. For example, you might have a case in which negligence figures prominently and want to find information about the subject matter. Imagine the staggering number of documents available on the Internet containing the word "negligence." Narrow your search to a more definitive term, adding the state in which the case occurred, as well as any other specific information required. As in the computerized legal research systems, it becomes necessary to experiment with key words so that the result is neither too broad nor too narrow.

If you want the exact wording to be included at the site, then type the material in quotation marks. For instance, if you were looking for the case of *Roe v. Wade,* you would put "Roe v. Wade" in the search so that only that exact case will be found. In some situations, using the links to legal sources is less time consuming than conducting your own search.

⊕ ASSIGNMENTS

1. Find this textbook on the Library of Congress web page. Make a copy of the page giving that information.

2. Using one of the links discussed in this Chapter, determine whether a homeowner may declare a homestead on a house that has been transferred to another individual. Where did you find that information?

   Answer: _____

   Web Site: _____

3. Find information about the Lemon Law at one of the consumer sites using one of the links provided. Define the law and list the site where the information was found.

   Definition: _____

   _____

   Web Site: _____

4. Find a law firm in your location that specializes in family law. List the name and address. _____

   _____

5. List the words you would use in a key word search to find the answer to the following question:

Are individuals who wish to solicit money for religious purposes protected under the United States Constitution if they wish to solicit at a

major shopping center? _____

_____

Key Words: _____

Why or why not may individuals solicit money for this purpose?

_____

_____

6. Prepare a simple will for JOANNE CASTRO, who lives in Your Town and Your State. She is single and has two children, a son JOSEPH CASTRO, who was born on May 5, 1996, and a daughter MARIA CASTRO, who was born on June 2, 1997. JOANNE CASTRO's address is: 1234 Sunset Avenue, Your City, Your State. Guardian for her children should she die before they reach the age of majority: her mother, MONICA CASTRO, residing at the same address. Her mother will also be designated as her Executor. Use one of the sources described in this chapter to prepare the will.

CHAPTER 4

Federal and State Sources

Contacting government agencies by telephone or regular mail is often difficult and time consuming. Spending the necessary time to reach the correct department or person is an arduous task. Most government agencies and departments are now available on the Web, and most give accurate and timely information on their sites. The federal courts, codes, and many cases are also available online. In this chapter, we will discuss the government agencies available online along with their functions. The organization of the federal courts will be explained and their sites given. You will learn how to find federal cases and statutes.

FEDERAL GOVERNMENT

Government Agencies

Government Sources. One of the most comprehensive listings of government sources on the Internet may be found at the Government Sources of Business and Economic Information at:

http://www.lib.umich.edu/00/inetdirrstacks/govdocs:tsangaustin

In addition to listing all government sources with web pages, it provides an evaluation of each. Bear in mind, however, that the evaluations are subjective and you may not agree with all assessments. However, with the number of government agencies establishing web pages, it is often useful to be able to read an evaluation prior to doing your own search.

Aviation.   Two government agencies are primarily responsible for information regarding airline accidents and incident reports. The National Transportation Safety Board (NTSB), located at:

http://www.ntsb.gov/aviation/aviation.htm

gives information helpful for aviation litigation, specifically information about airline crashes and incidents related to certain aircraft. Much of the information found on this page is available because of the Freedom of Information Act (FOIA). However, if requesting information via an FOIA form using regular mail, several weeks may pass before the information arrives. Much of the same information is available on the web site, shown in Figure 4-1.

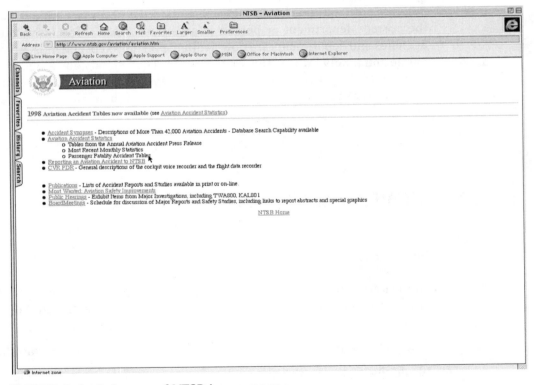

FIGURE 4-1   Subpage of NTSB home page

The Federal Aviation Administration (FAA), whose web page is located at:

http://www.faa.gov/

is responsible for the safety of civil aviation. As a component of the Department of Transportation, its functions include:

1. Regulating civil aviation to promote safety
2. Encouraging the development of air commerce and civil aeronautics
3. Developing and operating air traffic control and navigation systems for both civil and military aircraft
4. Developing and executing programs to control aircraft noise and other environmental effects of civil aviation
5. Regulating commercial space transportation[1]

Its activities include safety regulation of aircraft and airports, safe use of navigable airspace, construction or installation of visual and electronic aids to air navigation and their maintenance and operation, promotion of aviation safety abroad, regulation of commercial space transportation, and research and development of systems for a safe method of air navigation and air traffic control. The following additional information is available on the FAA's web site:

1. Agency policies
2. Regulations
3. Air traffic and safety
4. Regional offices and site maps
5. Commercial space transportation regulations
6. Civil aviation security

Both the NTSB's and FAA's sites are particularly helpful for those offices engaged in aviation litigation, particularly accident/incident reports and incidents involving certain types of aircraft and/or certain airlines.

Department of Transportation.   This federal department governs all transportation agencies of the government, including the FAA. At its web site, located at:

http://www.dot.gov/

---

[1] Federal Aviation Administration Web Page, **http://www.faa.gov/**

links are available to the other divisions within the department, including the following:

1. FAA
2. Federal Highway Administration
3. Federal Railroad Administration
4. Federal Transit Administration
5. Maritime Administration
6. National Highway Traffic Safety Administration
7. United States Coast Guard.

If the law office has a case that involves safety considerations on a federal highway or waterway, this site should be used.

State Department.   The Secretary of State is appointed by the President and is the chief foreign affairs adviser. He oversees the State Department, which is the senior executive department of the United States Government. Some of the activities of the Department include:

1. Advice on foreign policy
2. Negotiations in foreign affairs
3. Granting and issuing of passports
4. Negotiation, interpretation, and termination of treaties
5. Assuring protection of U.S. citizens, property and interests in foreign countries
6. Supervising immigration laws abroad
7. Providing information about travel conditions in foreign countries[2]

The State Department home page, shown in Figure 4-2, may be found at:

http://www.state.gov/index.html

This department also maintains a special page of travel advisories for individuals traveling to foreign countries, including those areas of political unrest or recent uprisings. The page is available at:

http://travel.state.gov/travel_warnings.html

---

2 United States State Department web page; **http://www.state.gov/index.html**

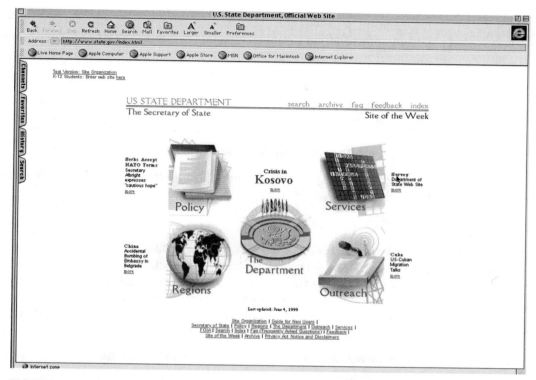

FIGURE 4-2 Official web site of the U.S. State Department

Consulting this page is particularly useful when traveling to a foreign country. It should always be checked before making travel reservations abroad.

United States Census Bureau. Statistical information gathered from the census is available on this site:

http://www.census.gov/

It includes census data, financial data for government, economic and population studies, and links to other sites.

Government Printing Office. Documents available from this office may be obtained from its web site at:

http://www.access.gpo.gov/

Information is available about the intelligence community, Congress, Office of the Special Counsel, General Accounting Office, Department of the Interior, Executive Office of the President, and various other departments.

The White House.   In order to find this site on the web, use the following address:

http://www2.whitehouse.gov/WH/Welcome.html

However, on many of the commercial services you may reach this site by merely keying:

white house

Information available at this site includes data on the President and Vice President, the history of the White House and tour information, a library of press releases, radio addresses, and other related web pages, summaries of today's press releases, the Constitution, and a considerable amount of material on current events. Cabinet offices and Executive Branch agencies are listed with addresses and telephone numbers at:

http://www.whitehouse.gov/WH/Cabinet/html/cabinet_links.html

Central Intelligence Agency.   The Director of the CIA heads the agencies that comprise the intelligence community of the United States. They conduct investigations, surveillance, research, and other activities. The web site is available at:

http://www.odci.gov/cia/

Their web site describes the functions of the agency as well as providing links to readings about the intelligence community.

Federal Bureau of Investigation.   The site for the FBI may be useful for those individuals who work in law offices that specialize in criminal law. Their web site is located at:

http://www.fbi.gov/

It includes information about the history of the FBI, programs available, speeches, press releases, chief investigations, the Most Wanted List, and other information.

Library of the House of Representatives.   An extensive law library, particularly valuable for federal sources, is available at the House of Representatives site at:

http://www.house.gov

The site also contains text of pending legislation as well as congressional testimony.

Immigration and Naturalization Service (INS).   This organization is an agency of the Department of Justice and is responsible for the admission, naturalization, stopping of illegal entry, and deportation of foreign nationals. Their Appeals Board hears appeals to deportation orders.

Immigration laws change rapidly. Anyone employed in the area of Immigration Law should consult the INS web site to obtain the latest rules and regulations. The web site also contains forms that would be used in this type of specialty practice. It can be found at:

http://www.ins.usdoj.gov

Department of Justice.   This department manages the legal business of the United States. All federal law enforcement agencies are within the DOJ. It represents the U.S. in civil and criminal cases, runs the federal prison system, and has departments that are responsible for immigration (see INS above), antitrust laws, civil rights laws, the FBI (see above), the Drug Enforcement Administration (DEA), and a number of other agencies. It is headed by the Attorney General of the United States. The web site, shown in Figure 4-3, is located at:

http://www.usdoj.gov

and includes information on the various agencies in the Department, recent case decisions involving the Justice Department, and other information related to the United States legal community.

Department of Commerce/Patent and Trademark Office.   Patent attorneys and paralegals will find this site particularly valuable for obtaining information about trademarks and patents. Forms are provided to register and maintain trademarks and patents. There are links to related sites. The site, shown in Figure 4-4, may be found at:

http://www.uspto.gov

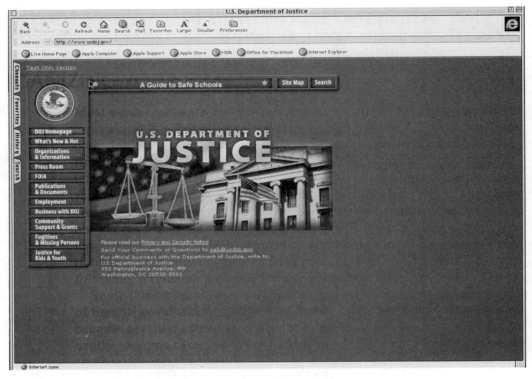

FIGURE 4-3 United States Department of Justice Home page

Internal Revenue Service.   A considerable amount of tax information is provided at the IRS's site at:

http://www.irs.ustreas.gov

Tax forms may be downloaded from the site. Publications on IRS regulations are also available for downloading.

Department of Labor.   The Department of Labor regulates working conditions, manpower development, and labor-management relations. Its web site contains information on wages, hours of employment, workplace issues, and running small businesses. It includes federal labor regulations and is located at:

http://www.dol.gov

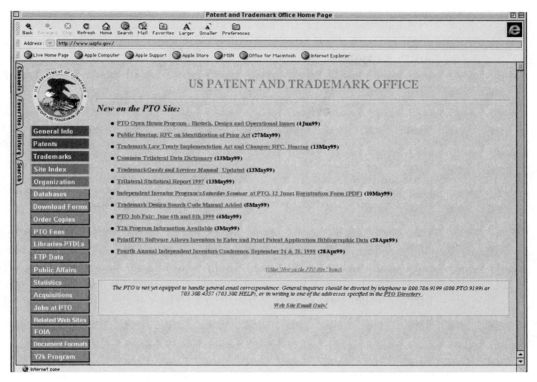

FIGURE 4-4   United States Patent and Trademark Office home page

Securities and Exchange Commission.   The SEC is responsible for ad-
ministering the federal and state laws that regulate the sale of securities.
The site includes the Securities Act of 1933, which requires the registration of securities to be sold to the public and the disclosure of complete
information to possible buyers; the Securities and Exchange Act of 1934,
which regulates both stock exchanges and sales of stock over the counter;
and a number of other laws related to the purchase and sale of securities
the SEC has the responsibility of enforcing. Its web site is particularly useful for those law offices specializing in corporate law and is located at:

http://www.sec.gov/

The web site provides a method for filing online, information on other corporate filings, a database to search for information on filings, information
for small businesses, and current rules and regulations.

An additional web site has been the center of a considerable amount of controversy and may not be available at the printing of this textbook. It is worth looking for, however, as it contains a data archive of electronic filings from the SEC's own database of corporate filings; it is located at:

http://www.town.hall.org/edgar/edgar.html

Social Security Administration.   Their web site provides the ability to access your own personal earnings and future benefits estimates. Information is provided about Social Security benefits and Medicare. Explanations are provided for the system's regulations. The site is available at:

http://www.ssa.gov/SSA_Home.html

Library of Congress.   Many additional departments and agencies exist in the federal government that are not listed here. For those departments not listed, the best place to find listings of federal, state and local governments and agencies is on the Library of Congress page, which provides links to other government departments. The page, shown in Figure 4-5, may be found at:

http://www.lcweb.loc.gov/

FEDERAL COURTS

The Federal courts are divided into the following general areas:

1. United States Supreme Court
2. Circuit Courts of Appeals
3. Federal District Courts

United States Supreme Court

The Supreme Court of the United States is the highest court in the land. It is located in Washington, D. C. and sits from the first Monday in October until the end of May. Nine justices sit on the court, one of whom is the Chief Justice, who presides over the Court. All decisions of the Federal Circuit Courts of Appeal may be appealed to the Supreme Court. It may also hear cases where the highest state court has issued a decision that challenges the validity of a federal law. Generally, the Court only hears

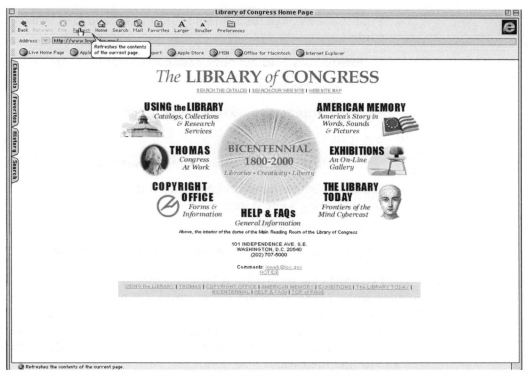

FIGURE 4-5   Home page of the Library of Congress

cases that raise significant issues and declines to hear the majority of cases
referred to it. Various web sites exist for different areas of the Supreme
Court as indicated:

1. Current court calendar

   http://supct.law.cornell.edu/supct/calendar.html

2. Oral arguments

   http://supct.law.cornell.edu/supct/argcal97.html

3. Case name search

   http://www.fedworld.gov/supcourt/csearch.htm

   This site is useful if you know the names of the parties to an action
   but do not have the complete citation.

4. FindLaw web page for Supreme Court cases and the United States Code

   http://www.findlaw.com/casecode/supreme.html

5. Cases from 1967–Present

   http://www.ljextra.com/cgi-bin/ussc

6. Supreme Court cases

   http://www.usscplus.com/research.shtml

   This site also includes oral arguments in Real Audio and the federal judiciary home page.

7. Supreme Court Rules

   http://www.law.cornell.edu/rules/supct/overview.html

The Federal Legal Information Through Electronics (FLITE) database includes over 7,000 Supreme Court cases from 1937-1975. Volumes 300-422 of the United States Reports are included in this database. If the case in which you are interested was decided during that time period, and you know the name and citation number, you may access the following web site to find the case:

http://www.fedworld.gov/supcourt/index.htm

If you would like to do a key word search and do not know the name or citation number of the case, use the following web site:

http://www.fedworld.gov/supcourt/fsearch.htm

Circuit Courts of Appeal

The intermediary federal courts for appeals is the Circuit Courts of Appeal, which hear cases appealed from the following United States District Courts. The thirteen circuits each represent several states and the federal system.

Twelve regional circuits represent intermediate courts of appeal. They hear appeals from the following United States District Courts in each state: Bankruptcy Courts, the Tax Court, and Administrative Agency Tribunal.

The United States Court of Appeals for the Federal Circuit represents federal appeals from the Court of Claims, Court of International Trade, Court of Veterans Appeals, Patents and Trademarks, and other courts with special jurisdiction. The number of judges in each Circuit varies by the size of the court and the number of cases being heard.

Several sources exist for finding cases from the Circuit Courts. General sources for all circuits may be found at:

http://www.law.vill.edu/Fed-Ct/fedcourt.html

This web page includes federal court opinions, Supreme Court rules, Appeals Court rules, and rules from some states and federal agencies.

FEDERAL COURT OPINIONS

Federal Circuit Courts of Appeal

A number of sources for finding opinions of the Circuit Courts are listed below:

http://search.ljx.com

http://www.ljextra.com/cgi-bin/cir

http://www.ll.georgetown.edu/Fed-Ct/Circuit/fed/search.html

http://www.law.emory.edu/fedcircuit/fedcasearch.html

http://www.law.vill.edu/Fed-Ct/fedcourt.html

Some law schools also have libraries online of appellate court opinions within individual districts:

1. First Circuit

    http://www.law.emory.edu/1circuit/

    http://www.law.emory.edu/1circuit/1casearch.html

2. Second Circuit

    http://www.tourolaw.edu/2ndcircuit/

    http://www.law.pace.edu/legal/us-legal/judiciary/second-circuit.html

3. Third Circuit

    http://www.law.vill.edu/Fed-Ct/ca03.html

4. Fourth Circuit

    http://www.law.emory.edu/4circuit/

5. Fifth Circuit

    http://www.ca5.uscourts.gov/www.law.utexas.edu/us5th/us5th.html

6. Sixth Circuit

    http://www.law.emory.edu/6circuit/

7. Seventh Circuit

    http://www.law.emory.edu/7circuit/7casearch.html

8. Eighth Circuit

    http://www.wulaw.wustl.edu/8th.cir/opinions.html

9. Ninth Circuit

    http://www.ce9.uscourts.gov

10. Tenth Circuit

    http://www.emory.edu/10circuit

11. Eleventh Circuit

    http://www.emory.edu/11circuit

12. Federal Circuit

    http://www.fedcir.gov/

    http://www.ll.georgetown.edu/Fed-Ct/Circuit/fed/

Some of these web sites also include District Court and Bankruptcy Court decisions for the specific circuits.

Federal District Courts

The United States District Courts are the trial courts on the federal level. There are ninety-four federal judicial districts, with at least one in each state. Larger and heavily populated states have several districts. Most cases heard in these courts involve questions of federal law, such as statutes, treaties, or the Constitution. Cases against the United States government, cases involving diversity of citizenship (where the plaintiff and defendant reside in different states and the amount in controversy is over $50,000), and cases in specialized areas such as customs and admiralty also come under the original jurisdiction of the District Courts. Federal crimes, such as racketeering, security fraud, bank robbery, mail fraud, certain drug-related crimes, and kidnapping, are also prosecuted in these courts.

The states generally list state court opinions and rules on the state court web pages. Therefore, the web pages will be listed below under each state's pages. A general web page for the Federal courts is available at:

http://www.uscourts.gov/

This page is the home page of the federal judiciary and includes information about the courts, opinions, and court news.

FEDERAL STATUTES

Federal Court Rules

The rules for the federal courts are available in the United States Codes, *supra*. The appendix to Title 28 of the United States Code contains the Federal Rules of Evidence, Appellate, and Civil Procedure. The appendix to Title 18 of the U.S. Code contains the Federal Rules of Criminal Procedure. The Federal Rules of Evidence are also found at:

http://www.law.cornell.edu/rules/fre/overview.html

Federal Rules of Civil Procedure

The Rules of Civil Procedure set out the procedural rules that must be followed in the federal courts. In this web page:

http://www.law.cornell.edu/rules/frcp/overview.htm

all of the rules and articles may be found by key word search. For example, if you are interested in specific filing requirements, use the key words "filing requirements Texas" and you should be able to reach the appropriate material. This web page also provides links to proposed changes in these rules as well as other documents that have been written about specific rules.

Web pages for specific Federal rules follow:

1. Federal Rules of Civil Procedure

   http://www.law.cornell.edu/rules/frcp/overview.html

2. Federal Rules of Evidence

   http://www.law.cornell.edu/rules/fre/overview.html

If the federal rule is confusing or obscure, use one of the treatises available:

1. *Moore's Federal Practice*—Federal courts
2. *Federal Practice and Procedure*—Federal courts practice
3. *McCormick on Evidence* or *Weinstein's Evidence*—Federal Rules of Evidence

Local federal court rules may be available at the Federal District Court web page for your state.

United States Code

The United States Code is arranged in Titles, beginning with the General Provisions (Title 1) and continuing alphabetically to the last title, which is War and National Defense (Title 50.) The web page to access all 50 titles may be found at:

http://www.law.cornell.edu/uscode/

Each code is further divided into various sections and chapters. This page enables one to search by several different methods, including the following:

1. Title and chapter
2. Title alone
3. By popular name of the law
4. By sections of the individual title
5. By table of contents to the Code

It should be noted that several different federal sources are available at the general Cornell Law site:

http://www.law.cornell.edu/

The Federal Rules of Civil Procedure are available on that site at:

http://www.law.cornell.edu/rules/frcp/overview.html

and the Federal Rules of Evidence may be accessed at:

http://www.law.cornell.edu/rules/fre/overview.html

Updating of the codes and rules is not generally accomplished in a timely fashion, so if the latest section is required, be sure to check the date and the advance sheets as well.

Federal Justices

Information about the Justices of the federal courts, as well as other information about the federal system, may be found at:

http://www.legal.gas.gov/

This is a general federal site that also provides information about statutes, regulations, state laws, professional associations, arbitration, mediation, and links to other legal sites.

STATE SOURCES

State Government Offices

The number of web sites available that provide information on state government offices is very large. Instead of providing web page addresses for all fifty states, the web pages that provide links to the different states are included below. These particular links supply information about not only state government offices, but also statutes, law reviews, publishers, and other material.

One of the most comprehensive sites for this purpose is:

http://www.findlaw.com/

This source provides a great number of sources for legal research, including the following:

1. Federal government sources
2. Legal news

3. Law reviews

4. Statutes

5. Law schools

6. Cases

7. Professional legal organizations

8. Experts in various specialty fields

9. International legal sources

One source that has a relatively fast method of linking to state and federal law sources, including state codes, is:

http://www.lawsonline.com/

State Courts and Cases

Many different state courts have their own web pages. A site where links to those state courts, as well as the court opinions, may be found is located at:

http://www.law.vill.edu/State-Ct/index.html

Another excellent link to material on the web is the World Wide Web Virtual Law Library, which can be found at:

http://www.law.indiana.edu/law/v-lib/lawindex.html

Not only does this library provide information on state sources, but it also provides links to many different specialty areas of the law, including business law, family law, labor law, torts, taxation, criminal law, and many others. It links to other sites listing additional legal resources available on the Web. In some cases, this library provides an excellent starting point for legal research on the Web.

Some additional sites that provide links and indexes to state law on the Internet follow:

http://law.house.gov/17.htm

http://www.prairienet.org/~scruffy/f.htm

http://www.law.indiana.edu/law/v-lib/states.html

State of California. California provides an extensive number of Internet sites for state government information, codes, and cases. Some of the more noteworthy of these sites follow:

1. California Legislative Information—**http://www.leginfo.ca.gov/ index.htm**
   This site provides all legislative information for California with links to bills, laws, the State Legislature, and publications.
2. California Codes—**http://www.leginfo.ca.gov/calaw.html**
   This site includes all 29 codes of the State of California.
3. California Courts—**http://www.courtinfo.ca.gov/**
   This site includes court opinions from the state courts, Judicial Council forms, court rules, information concerning branch courts, structure of the California judicial system, and provides an online guide to the California courts with information about Family, Juvenile, Criminal, Small Claims, and Traffic Court, as well as alternative dispute resources, jury duty, and legal resource links.
4. Statutes and regulations—**http://www.ca.gov/s/govt/govcode.html**
   In addition to providing all 29 California Codes, this site enables you to do a subject and key word search for the appropriate code section. Links to the California Code of Regulations, State Constitution, California bills, and United States Codes are provided.
5. California Secretary of State—**http://www.ss.ca.gov/**
   The Secretary of State's site provides information about business programs in the state, state archives with historic records on state government, campaign reports, and notary information.

State of Washington.   The State Attorney General's Office site at:

http://www.wa.gov/ago/

provides links to Attorney General opinions, consumer protection, lemon law, and antitrust regulations. It also provides information on issues such as the environment, the death penalty, utility rates, and tobacco litigation.

CITATIONS

All cases have their own "address," known as a citation. The citation gives the volume number, series, and page number on which the case is located. For example, 45 U.S. 222 may be found in Volume 45 of United States Reports at page 222.

The proper methods of citing cases may be found in an online textbook located at:

www.law.cornell.edu/citation/citation.table.html

SHEPARDIZING

Shepard's lists relevant cases and other material that occur after a case decision is handed down from the courts and that have a direct bearing on that particular statute or case. It lists all subsequent cases that cite the subject case. It tells whether a case has been followed or overruled, which is the most critical notation. If you are preparing a legal document for the courts and are citing relevant cases to support your point of view, it is critical that the cases cited have not been overruled.

In *Shepard's* the subject case may be found by looking in the appropriate volumes for that particular series, then numerically by volume, then by page number. *Shepard's* lists almost every case and statute in the United States. "Shepardizing" refers to the determination of whether the subject case has been overruled by a later case by looking it up in *Shepard's Citations*. *Shepard's* is also useful for tracing the history of the case. Information on *Shepard's* is available online at:

http://shepards.com/ccentral/tutorial/content1.htm

WESTLAW AND LEXIS

These all-encompassing computerized legal research systems are also available online for a fee. They may be accessed on the Internet via their respective web pages. You must enter your password to gain access to the database; your time using the database is computed automatically. These sites are available at:

http://www.westlaw.com

http://www.lexis.com

Additional sources are also available on the web pages. For instance, *West's Legal Directory of Attorneys* may be accessed through the address above.

PLEADINGS AND FORMS

A number of different sites make forms and documents available on the Web. In addition, many attorneys who have their own web pages provide documents and forms, some free and some for a fee. Some forms may be obtained from the West web site at:

http://www.westlaw.com

or

http://www.westlegalstudies.com

California uses many Judicial Council Forms that are available on the state websites and the following site as well:

http://www.LawCA.com/JC.htm

Again, some of these forms and documents are free; and others are charged for. The latter web site provides the ability to download forms from the site itself. Some legal areas whose associated forms are available at this site include:

1. Name change
2. Eviction
3. Orders
4. Dissolution
5. Bankruptcy

Some of the federal sites described in this Chapter also provide links to sites that provide forms and documents.

A general site for legal forms may be accessed at:

http://www.washlaw.edu/

SUMMARY

In this Chapter we reviewed the substantive research encountered in a legal environment. Different federal and state offices and agencies were discussed, both the state and federal courts were described, and links were provided to government agencies, courts, cases, and statutes.

The basic sources for a legal research assignment are included in this Chapter. The advantages and disadvantages of WESTLAW and LEXIS were reviewed, and online sources for various types of primary sources were furnished.

⊕ ASSIGNMENTS

1. Find the Codes for your state and indicate their Internet address below:

   _____

   _____

2. Are the court decisions from the Appellate and Supreme Courts of your state included on the Web? If so, indicate the addresses of their web pages. _____

   _____

   _____

3. Find the Federal statute that indicates the definition of "racketeering." Indicate the web page address of this definition as well as the definition itself. _____

   _____

   _____

4. Does your state recognize capital punishment? If so, under what circumstances? In addition to the answers, indicate the web page where the information was found.

   _____

   _____

5. List five government offices in your state that have web pages. What are these agencies' functions?

   _____

   _____

   _____

6. Find the web page for the U.S. State Department. Describe the duties and responsibilities of the Secretary of State.

_____

_____

CHAPTER 5

Secondary Sources

In the previous Chapters we learned about the primary sources (primary authority) used for research in the federal and state areas of information. By definition, primary sources represent the "law" in your particular jurisdiction. They consist of authority that is binding on the courts and include laws (codes and statutes), court decisions, administrative regulations, constitutions, and other sources of law as opposed to interpretive or indirect information from legal encyclopedias, treatises, textbooks, or other secondary sources.

Secondary sources are useful for learning about the law and finding other material as well as locating primary sources. They represent persuasive authority that a judge or justice might use, but is not required to. Such sources include legal encyclopedias and cases or statutes from other jurisdictions. For example, in deciding a case in California, a judge may look at persuasive authority on the laws of other states; however, he must use cases in his jurisdiction in California in reaching a decision.

Secondary sources may be found online in law library and college library catalogs. In some cases, legal encyclopedias are available for online search. Law review articles often provide useful information and citations to cases in your own jurisdiction.

LAW SCHOOLS AND THEIR LIBRARIES

The complete list of law schools and their libraries available online is too large to put into a book format. It is advisable to do your own search for law schools and their libraries if the particular school is not listed here. In most cases, the site address for the law school and its library are listed as separate sites. The law school sites will provide particular information about individual law schools, such as academic services, faculty, placement activities, courses offered, and admissions requirements. Individual law school sites will provide links to their own libraries.

Case Western Reserve University—Ohio

Both the law school and its library are available online. To go directly to the law school, find:

http://lawwww.cwru.edu/

and to go directly to the library, find:

http://lawwww.cwru.edu/cwrulaw/library/libinfo.html

In addition to general information about the law school itself, the law school site provides links to other legal reference materials, as well as publications and research by the law school students and professors.

The library page provides a guide to Case Western's law library as well as online catalogs of library materials, links to other law school libraries, and the location of their basic legal research information.

Chicago-Kent College of Law/Library

This law school and library offers one of the best sites for finding links and information about any of the law libraries available online. In addition to providing information about its own law school, links to various county departments are included. Their law review is available online, and decisions of the Illinois Human Rights Commission are provided.

The law school is available at:

http://www.kentlaw.edu/

Cornell University—Law School/Library

Perhaps the largest provider of links to applicable legal research sites, Cornell provides their law school web page as well as sites for the law library and the Legal Information Institute. Their addresses are:

Law school: **http://www.law.cornell/edu/admit/admit.htm**

Law library: **http://www.law.cornell.edu/library/default.html**

Legal Information Institute: **http://www.law.cornell.edu:80/lii.
table.html**

The law school provides a great deal of information about the school as well as law reviews and studies undertaken at the law school. The law library's page supplies an extensive legal research encyclopedia, a Global Legal Information Network dealing with international law sources, research guides, and law journals.

The Legal Information Institute provides links to various government agency web pages and has one of the largest number of legal research links available. This is an excellent point to begin your legal research. Access to the Supreme Court's most recent decisions are also available at this site. The decisions may be accessed through four search methods:

1. The full citation
2. A topical index
3. A key word search
4. Indices of the names of parties by the year of the decision
5. By date of decision (for the most recent term only)

A gallery of the Supreme Court Justices is provided, with biographical information and pictures of all of the justices, along with links to the opinions written by each justice, including concurring and dissenting opinions.

Emory University—Law School/Library

This site provides access to links to many federal circuit court decisions and other documents available on the Web. It also provides information on legal materials in Georgia and a research aid as well.

The law school may be found at:

http://www.law.emory.edu/

and the library at:

http://www.law.emory.edu/LAW/library.html

Harvard Law School/Library

Most of the information on this site relates to the law school itself. Very few links are provided to enable other research capabilities. The law school site gives extensive information about classes, professors, admissions, alumni, students, and special events. The library site gives information primarily about sources available at Harvard itself. The sites may be found at:

Law school: **http://www.law.harvard.edu/**

Law library: **http://www.law.harvard.edu/library/**

Indiana University Law School/Library

An excellent source for a tremendous amount of legal research materials and links is available at:

http://www.law.indiana.edu

This site is updated frequently and can be depended on to generally have current information as well as the most current links available.

University of Chicago Law School/D'Angelo Law Library

A considerable amount of information about both the law school and many law sites are available at this site. It is also home to the Center for the Study of Constitutionalism in Eastern Europe. It contains links to many federal sources, including cases, courts, and government agencies. The sites are found at:

School: **http://www-law.lib.uchicago.edu/**

Library: **http://www-law.lib.uchicago.edu/lib/**

Space and purpose considerations do not allow the listing of every law library with web sites in this volume. However, most major law schools in the United States provide web sites for both their schools and libraries. If a law school is not listed here, then conduct a search of law schools to find the one you are looking for.

LEGAL DICTIONARY

Legal dictionaries are online, as well as other secondary sources. A good site to look for words with definitions organized both alphabetically and numerically is:

http://www.thelawofice.com/Research/LawDict.htm

Another legal dictionary available online that provides definitions for words on a worldwide basis may be found at:

http://www.islandnet.com/~wwlia/diction/html

LEGAL RESEARCH QUESTIONS————————————

Encyclopedia Britannica

While this encyclopedia is not a legal encyclopedia *per se,* it does contain thousands of sources of interest. It identifies the best sites in hundreds of subject areas and is available at:

http://www.eBLAST.com/

WESTLAW

Users of the WESTLAW service have their own listserv, available by subscription by sending an e-mail to:

listserv@lawlib.wuacc.edu

Subject: **(any)**

Message: **subscribe westlawuser-l Jlong (or your screen name)**

WESTLAW users discuss pertinent issues and items related to the WESTLAW data base.

Past discussions may be found at:

http://www.ftplaw.wuacc.edu/listproc/westlawuser-l/

Information about a subscription to WESTLAW may be obtained at:

http://www.westlaw.com

which is the official site for WESTLAW. You may also access WEST-
LAW from this site if you have an existing account.

Legal Search Engines

In order to find a site that provides a number of different search engines to
other legal information, go to:

http://www.dreamscape.com/frankvad/search.legal.html

Law-Related LISTSERVS

As discussed earlier, listservs represent a means for an individual to subscribe to a discussion group that sends e-mail out to a number of people
about different topics. Once you have subscribed to the listserv, your
e-mail address becomes part of the listserv's database. When someone
sends out an e-mail to the list, all members receive a copy. If you wish to
respond to the e-mail, a reply is sent to the group. Often valuable information may be obtained about legal issues.

For instance, when the author was writing this textbook, she asked the
members of the paralegal educators' listserv about legal links they may
have used and found to be valuable in their teaching of legal research.
Many of these suggestions are included here.

One particularly valuable listserv actually contains lists of other
listservs, journals, law firms on the net, and bulletin boards that might be
of interest to the legal profession. One may join this listserv by sending an
e-mail with the following information:

TO: **listserv@justice.eliot.me.us**

FROM: <your screen name>

SUBJECT: legal list

BODY: Subscribe LEGAL-LIST <your screen name>

Once you join any listserv, you will continue getting all e-mail distributed on the listserv until you unsubscribe. After you join, an e-mail will be
sent to you with information on how to post messages and how to

unsubscribe. Be sure to keep this e-mail in your files in the event you decide at some future time that you are no longer interested in receiving e-mail from the list.

An excellent source for obtaining lists of all accessible legal listservs is available at:

http://www.kentlaw.edu/lawlinks/listservs.html

This site provides information about over 400 legal lists that you may join as well as a number of different newsgroups on legal topics.

One particularly valuable list is aimed at the exchange of information about law-related Internet resources. Subscribing to this list will assure the receipt of every announcement of new or updated law-related resources. Discussions are also provided on the merits of various sites and questions asked and answered about how to find a particular topic. If you do a considerable amount of legal research on the Internet and wish to keep abreast of all the latest developments on new sites, it would be beneficial to join this list. The following e-mail will enter a subscription to this list:

TO: **listserv@listserv.law.cornell.edu**

FROM: <your screen name>

SUBJECT: list <or any other topic>

BODY: Subscribe LAWSRC-L <your screen name>

One relatively new list that is comprised primarily of attorneys who are new to using the Internet for legal research is called NET-LAWYERS. Individuals share their discoveries of new sites and critique various sites. People ask and answer questions about where to find certain items. Although the site is largely made by and for attorneys, it is valuable for anyone who does legal research on the Internet and may be joined by sending the following e-mail:

TO: **net-lawyers-request@webcom.com**

FROM: <your screen name>

BODY: Subscribe <your screen name>

CHAPTER 6

Specialized Topics

This Chapter will describe some of the more common areas of specialty for law offices and, in each section, list and describe the sites related to those particular topics. A personal search may yield additional sites, particularly since new web pages appear daily. One excellent source to begin your search for specialty areas is called "Legal Links," and is located at:

http://www.amicus.ca/links.html

This site provides excellent information for paralegals looking for specific practice areas or background information on a legal-related topic. Students or paralegals unfamiliar with the specialized practice area are wise to use this site for resources. It is also useful for those situations where one requires more than the usual federal and state links available at other sites. Practice areas included herein are:

1. Civil litigation
2. Family law
3. Probate law
4. Real property law
5. Business, corporate, and securities law
6. Tax law
7. Personal injury
8. Health and disability

9. Bankruptcy

10. Insurance law

11. Constitutional law

12. Civil rights

13. Labor and employment law

14. Environmental law

Other non-law-related links provided on this page include information on Internet law, hardware and software, help with using the Internet, tips on searches and e-mail, and even assistance with web-site construction.

Another excellent source for beginning a search for legal resources, legal services, or attorneys by specialty area is the Law Around the Net site located at:

http://www.law.net/roundnet.html

This site provides a drop-down list through which you may search. Their legal resources section provides access to courts, government offices, schools, and many other sources. The legal services area provides links to appraisers, bail bonding, court reporters, expert witnesses, paralegals, private investigation, and many others. A copy of their web page is included below as Figure 6-1.

BANKRUPTCY

Title 11 of the United States Code contains the bankruptcy laws, which are federal statutes. It provides for a plan for a debtor who is unable to pay his creditors, to resolve his debts by dividing his assets among his creditors. Some bankruptcy proceedings allow a debtor to stay in business using income that is forthcoming, to pay his/her debts. Bankruptcy law allows debtors to discharge the financial obligations they have accumulated, after their assets are distributed, even if their debts have not been fully paid off.

Proceedings in bankruptcy are supervised and litigated in the United States Bankruptcy Courts, which are a part of the Federal District Courts. United States Trustees handle the supervisory and administrative responsibilities of the proceedings. These proceedings are governed by the Bankruptcy Rules established by the United States Supreme Court.

The most common type of bankruptcy proceeding is a Chapter 7 (liquidation), which requires the appointment of a trustee, who gathers the

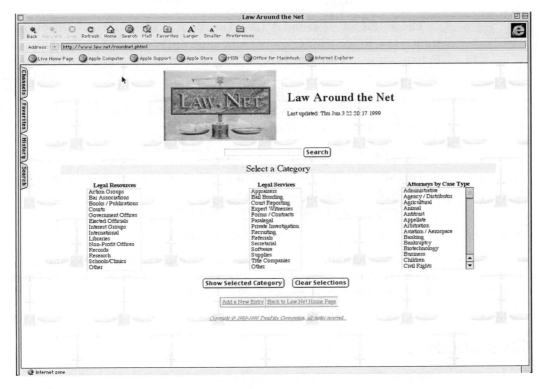

FIGURE 6-1   Law around the Net web site

debtor's property that is not exempt, sells it, and pays the creditors from the proceeds. Chapter 11, 12 and 13 proceedings enable the debtor to develop a plan for paying his creditors over a period of time.

The official Federal Judiciary home page is:

http://www.uscourts.gov/

By using "bankruptcy" as a key word to search on this page, information about the bankruptcy courts may be obtained. Bankruptcy filings are also accessible from this page, as well as news about the bankruptcy courts. Links are provided to the bankruptcy courts in the various states as well.

As discussed above, the FindLaw site is an excellent source for many specialty areas of law, including bankruptcy. Again, this site is found at:

http://www.findlaw.com

The FindLaw Consumer Law Center provides information on bankruptcy law for consumers, an explanation of the types of bankruptcy, links to bankruptcy courts, bankruptcy law information, and links to attorneys who specialize in bankruptcy law. There are also links to federal bankruptcy court sites, listing their decisions.

Definitions of bankruptcy law and links to the bankruptcy courts in the different states may be found at:

http://www.cornell.edu/topics/archive/bankruptcy.html

This site includes court decisions and Bankruptcy Code provisions (Title 11 of the United States Code.)

An Internet Bankruptcy Library is provided at:

http://bankrupt.com/

This site contains news, publications, resource materials, an online directory of bankruptcy clerks, consumer bankruptcy issues, and links to other bankruptcy resources.

CIVIL RIGHTS

The civil rights laws relate to the rights of citizens guaranteed by the United States Constitution, including freedom of speech, freedom of association, and freedom of religion. The civil rights amendments to the Constitution (the 13th, 14th and 15th) deal with slavery, discrimination, and the right to vote. The Civil Rights Acts are federal laws relating to the prohibition of discrimination based on race, color, age, sex, religion, or national origin.

Attorneys who practice in this legal specialty area generally also specialize in Constitutional Law. One of the major organizations in this area is the American Civil Liberties Union, (ACLU), which is a nonpartisan, nonprofit public-interest organization that is devoted to protecting the rights of all individuals. Their web page may be found at:

http://www.aclu.org/

A considerable amount of information is available on their web page, including the following:

1. Information about the organization
2. Issues of church and state

3. Criminal justice issues

4. Death penalty information

5. Rights of immigrants

6. Gay rights

7. Women's rights

8. Racial equality

9. Voting rights

10. Lie detector testing

11. Drug testing and the work environment

A number of other topical issues related to civil rights and liberties are also included in this web page.

The civil rights provisions of the United States Code are available at:

http://www.cornell.edu/uscode/42/ch21.html

An extensive site that was established by the University of Minnesota Law School with database search capabilities provided by West Publishing, is located at:

http://www.umn.edu/humanrts/

This site focuses on important human rights–related international treaties, as well as other materials, with authoritative citations provided. Links are given for the Human Rights Commission, the Inter-American Court of Human Rights Organization on Security and Cooperation in Europe, Resource Information Center, INS Asylum Branch, and information about sessions of the United Nations Commission on Human Rights.

CONSUMER LAW

Several online libraries exist with information on consumer law. These libraries provide links to a vast amount of information about the rights of consumers:

http://www.fis.utoronto.ca/~tjaden/consumer.htm

http://www.findout.com/leglib.htm

The National Fraud Information Center in Washington, D.C., provides a web site to allow consumers a method for reporting fraud. These reports are referred to the fraud database, administered by the Federal Trade Commission, the FBI, the Secret Service, the SEC, United States Attorneys, and postal inspectors. The site is located at:

http://www.fraud.org/

INTELLECTUAL PROPERTY/COPYRIGHT LAW

Intellectual property and copyright laws are in a state of flux in relation to the Internet. Experts differ as to the extent the copyright laws cover the Internet itself in relation to copying material from web pages. New laws are expected to be developed in this area.

The United States Copyright Office maintains its own web site at:

http://www.lcweb.loc.gov/copyright/

This site contains an extensive amount of material on copyright law, including the law itself. Other items that may be found on this page include:

1. Speeches and press releases
2. Publications and information about the office itself
3. Copyright registration and application forms
4. Brochures on the copyright process
5. Conducting a search on copyright records
6. Links to other pages on copyright law
7. Federal regulations related to copyright law

The Copyright Clearance Center provides information about copyright licenses for a wide variety of copyright holders and may be found at:

http://www.copyright.com/

CORPORATE LAW

Corporate law is an area of business law that concerns the making and dissolution of corporations. It includes tax law, dealings with the Securities and Exchange Commission (SEC), and preparation of corporate formation and dissolution documentation.

Information about large government contracts can be found at the Commerce Business Daily site. It lists abstracts of proposed contracts on a daily basis. This site is located at:

http://www.ld.com/cbd/

A description of limited liability companies and how they operate may be found at:

http://www.lic-usa.com/

This site includes key documents used in the formation of these companies as well as the parts of the Internal Revenue Code that relate to this type organization.

A site for locating all state home pages for their Secretaries of State is found at:

http://www.plains.uwyo.edu/~prospects/secstate.html

A number of databases may be accessed via links provided on this page:

1. Nonprofit corporations
2. Charities databases
3. UCC
4. Trademarks
5. State government offices relating to corporations

Several states' Business and Professions Codes are available via links to the following site:

http://www.law.cornell.edu/topics/statestatutes.html#business

Dun & Bradstreet provides information on more than 60,000 companies with web sites:

http://www.companiesonline.com/

Blue Sky Laws (securities regulations) are available at:

http://www.law.ab.umd.edu/marshall/bluesky/

This site includes state orders regulating securities offerings on the Internet, Uniform Securities Act, state laws and cases, and links to Federal Securities agencies and federal law.

The complete Securities Act of 1933 may be found at:

http://www.law.uc.edu/CCL/33Act/Index.html

The SEC maintains its own site at:

http://www.sec.gov/

There is a considerable amount of information about the SEC itself on this site, as well as laws and regulations related to the transfer of shares of stock.

CRIMINAL LAW

The practice of criminal law involves the prosecution of individuals accused of crimes and their defense. Prosecutors are generally district attorneys and assistant district attorneys employed by the government. Defense attorneys may be either public defenders employed by the government or private attorneys. An excellent source for information about criminal law is the FindLaw site described and pictured above.

The Institute for Law and Justice in Virginia provides links to criminal justice sites at:

http://www.ilj.org/#favorite

In addition to providing research and consulting services related to criminal justice, this site provides links to government agencies and various criminal sub-specialty areas such as substance abuse, corrections, sentencing, juvenile justice, courts, federal and state court decisions, and state and federal criminal codes: a very inclusive page of links in the area of criminal law.

A site providing information about the criminal laws of Canada is located at:

http://www.firstlinelaw.com/

Information on this site is useful to individuals facing criminal charges in Canada or those who have a general interest in how the Canadian criminal legal process works. Detailed information is provided about the criminal process, including arrest, charge, bail, pleas, court, trial, jury, sentencing, appeals, pardons, and other similar data. A picture of the First Line Criminal Law web page is included herein as Figure 6-2.

Another page that provides a number of links to other pages in the area of criminal law is located at:

http://www.payles.com/law/criminal.html

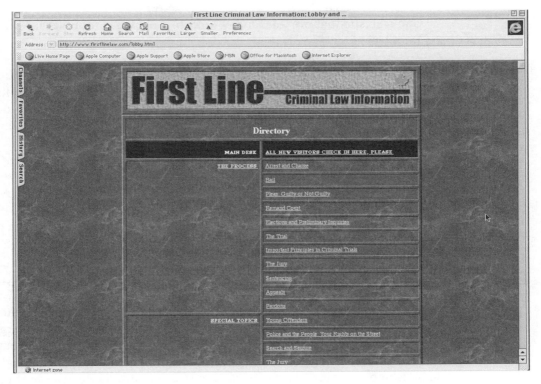

FIGURE 6-2   First Line criminal law information web page

Included are sites about criminal justice, criminal defense, defense litigation, constitutions, statutes, codes, Supreme Court decisions, noteworthy criminal decisions, prison law, uniform crime reports, search and seizure issues, and sentencing.

ELDER LAW

Elder law actually encompasses many other specialty areas of law and is growing rapidly. Senior citizens are the largest and fastest-growing group in the United States. Along with becoming a senior citizen comes a whole raft of legal problems and needs, from health issues to estate planning; from issues of entitlement, to Social Security, disability, Medicare, and Medicaid; making of wills, probating estates, and other legal issues encountered by the elderly.

One web site that provides many links to web pages for elder law may be found at:

http://www.catalaw.com/topics/Elder/html

Links are provided to sites about health and welfare, disability, wills, trusts, and estates; and national sites including elder care information and senior law. Elder law links are also provided for Canada and Australia.

The Senior Law home page is located at:

http://www.seniorlaw.com

This page supplies information about Medicare, Medicaid, elder law, estate planning, and the rights of the elderly. Links to court decisions, elder abuse statutes, estate planning, and other law resources are provided.

ENVIRONMENTAL LAW

The area of environmental law is one of the fastest growing in the United States today. Air and water pollution are of major concern in our large metropolitan areas. Both the Federal government and state governments have established many environmental regulations for companies and individuals to protect the environment. One site that offers information about environmental issues all over the world is located at:

http://www.econet.apc.org/scripts/wwwwais/cnfig=envlaw

It provides links to a number of resources in the Western Hemisphere in particular, including North America, South America, and Central America. It also has links to sites pertaining to environmental law in Europe, Asia, and Africa. This site has been provided by the Environmental Law Alliance Worldwide in their United States office.

The Worldwide Web Virtual Library has a central site for many environmental law resources. This site is an excellent place to start for a search of environmental law issues, and may be found at:

http://www.law.indiana.edu/

The International Earth Science Information Network Consortium operates a data center for the National Aeronautics and Space Administration (NASA). Their site provides information from the World Conservation Union, United Nations Environment Program, World Resources Institute, and the British Columbia Ministry of Environment, Land, and Parks. The site includes many environmental treaties and agreements, including World treaties for the protection of the environment. The site may be found at:

http://www.sedac.ciesin.org/pidb/pidb-home.html

A number of government agencies are devoted to the preservation of the environment, including the following, whose purposes are indicated along with their web pages:

1. Environmental Protection Agency—**http://www.epa.gov/**
    The EPA is located in Washington, D.C. and is an agency of the federal government.
2. U. S. Geological Survey—**http://www.usgs.gov/**
    This federal agency is devoted to geological issues, as well as mapping and water preservation.
3. Wetlands Regulation Center—**http://www.wetlands.com/regs/**
    This site, sponsored by the Environmental Technical Services Company in Austin, Texas, provides the provisions of the Clean Water Act for the preservation of wetlands and our waterways.

ESTATE PLANNING

Estate planning involves preparation of wills and other estate plans for clients, probate, and the preparation of trusts. Probate statutes for many states may be found at:

http://www.law.cornell.edu/topics/statestatutes.html#probate

A large collection of information about resources devoted to the area of trusts and estates may be found at the United States House of Representatives' site at:

http://www.law.house.gov/112.htm

FAMILY LAW

Family law includes all law that deals with families, including divorce, dissolution, child custody, child support, visitation, adoption, child welfare, and domestic violence. The most common area in law offices is divorce or dissolution.

An excellent site that provides information on divorce, property issues, child custody, and child support is provided at:

http://www.nolo.com/fam.html#2

This site is presented by Nolo Press, which is well known for its publishing of self-help books in many areas of law. The site provides discussion of custody agreements, divorce, tax planning, property issues, and many other subjects that must be considered when obtaining a divorce.

A number of issues related to divorce are covered at:

http://www.divorcenet.com/

Issues of cohabitation, custody, visitation, status of grandparents, military divorce, paternity, and other related matters are discussed.

The World Wide Web Virtual Law Library provides a number of family law resources at:

http://www.law.indiana.edu/law/v-lib/family.html

and the statutes in the area of domestic relations are provided for a number of states at:

http://www.law.cornell.edu/topics/statestatutes.html#family

The United States Office of Child Support Enforcement provides information about this issue, as well as links to the state's sites, at:

http://www.acf.dhhs.gov/ACFPrograms/CSE/

A site that provides information about divorce laws in all fifty states may be found at:

http://www.divorcenet.com/fla-state.html

A number of links to issues related to domestic violence may be found at:

http://www.ocs.mq.edu.au/~korman/feminism/dv.html

IMMIGRATION LAW

The Immigration and Naturalization Service (INS) is a federal agency that handles the admission, naturalization, and deportation of foreign nationals. (See the previous description under the sections on government agencies in

Chapter 4.) It is also responsible for the prevention of illegal entry of nonresident aliens. Its web site may be found at:

http://www.ins.doj.gov

The American Immigration Center provides self-help for immigration services. It has information packages concerning emigration of families, visas, employment, green cards, citizenship, and student visas. It provides a number of links to other immigration law sites; document preparation assistance is furnished; and immigration forms may be downloaded from this site. The link to immigration law gives information on the following:

1. Filing fees for immigration application forms
2. Adjustment of status
3. New laws
4. Dual nationality
5. Fingerprint requirements
6. Medical vaccinations
7. Affidavit of support forms
8. Facilitation of legal entry
9. Interior enforcement
10. Concise explanation of immigration laws
11. Links to forms required

The site may be found at:

http://us-immigration.com/

The site for American Immigration Resources on the Net is located at

http://www.wave.net/upg/immigration/resource.html

Information provided on this site includes:

1. Links to United States immigration laws
2. Regulations and procedures
3. Immigration lawyers and organizations
4. Extensive links to related laws
5. Sampson bill
6. INS home page

7. State Department visa information

8. Immigration forms

9. Immigration Nationality and Citizenship law

10. Case law

11. State Department immigration information

12. Foreign student immigration issues

The Immigration Superhighway page is a vast resource providing information and links to most relevant material in the immigration field. It is located at:

http://www.immigration-usa.com/i_suphwy.html

Information on the following topics may be found therein:

1. Immigration forum

2. Immigration and nationality act

3. Changing status and extending visits

4. Obtaining a green card

5. How to change status to permanent residence

6. Eligibility for visas

7. Foreign student immigration status

8. Diversity immigrant visa lottery

9. Cuban legal immigration program

10. American visas for investors and treaty traders

11. Immigration forms

12. Articles of interest in many immigration topics

A helpful site for immigrants wishing to assimilate into the American lifestyle is provided at:

http://www.buildingyourself.com/immig.htm

Helpful hints are given at this site in the areas of:

1. Keys to understanding and adjusting to American life.

2. Links to sites connected to employment, business, public service, transportation, government, immigration and citizenship.

LITIGATION/PERSONAL INJURY LAW———————————

Because the laws related to civil litigation are primarily state laws, see the above sections in Chapter 4 on methods of finding the laws for your state. For the federal laws, see the section in Chapter 4 that discusses federal law. Some specialized sites for managing cases in civil litigation and personal injury will be provided here and may be used for state or federal cases.

Sometimes these suits involve defendants who are large corporations. Hoovers Online compiles data on public companies, in order to facilitate finding information about a company, including its history and financial condition. Hoovers may be found at:

http://www.hoovers.com

Conducting an investigation into both locating people and their records is another aspect of civil litigation. In addition to the web sites discussed above, specific sources available for this purpose include the following:

1. People and businesses

   http://www.databaseamerica.com

   http://www.four11.com

   http://www.switchboard.com

2. Motor vehicle records

   http://www.knowx.com

   (fee based); for a nominal fee, public records and motor vehicle information are available.

3. Links to motor vehicle records

   http://www.inil.com/users/dguss/wgator.htm

Cases against automobile manufacturers for defective products represents another specialty within personal injury law. The National Highway Traffic Safety Administration (NHTSA) maintains its own site providing data on traffic safety, including problems and complaints with different automobiles. It may be accessed at:

http://www.nhtsa.dot.gov

This site includes links to other databases, including:

1. *Technical Services Bulletins.* Automobile manufacturers provide bulletins to repair facilities on the repair of problems reported by car owners.

2. *Consumer Complaints.* A database of all complaints by consumers is provided here. Trends of particular problems with cars are noted.

3. *Recalls.* A separate database is maintained for those automobiles that have been recalled. Vehicle owners are notified of recalls that affect vehicle safety.

4. *Investigations.* The National Highway Traffic Safety Administration initiates its own investigations after many consumers have complained about the same problem with an automobile. Results of these investigations are available. Before doing research on this site, be sure to note the model, make, year, and suspected problem with the vehicle.

Similar data for other consumer products is available at the Consumer Product Safety Commission's site at:

http://www.cpsc.gov

Descriptions of products that have been recalled are provided, as well as press releases and other information valuable to consumers. If your practice is primarily involved with products liability actions, then you may wish to subscribe to the Consumer Product Safety Commission's listserv. You will be sent (via e-mail) safety information and product recalls. To subscribe to this service, send the following e-mail message:

TO: **listproc@cpsc.gov**
FROM: <your screen name>
BODY: sub CPSCINFO-L <your screen name>

Another aspect of the civil litigation position in personal injury is the reading of medical records and calculation of damages. The value of a suit is directly related to an understanding of the extent of medical injuries incurred by the plaintiff. A thorough understanding of reading medical records assists in this process. An excellent site for this purpose is located at:

http://www.sun2.lib.uci.edu/HSG/HSGuide.html

This site gives links to multimedia tutorials that may be accessed on-line. Links are also provided to articles and textbooks on various medical topics.

A similar site is located at the Virtual Medical Center at:

http://www.medhelp.org

Links on this site give categories for injuries.

If information is needed on the effects of certain prescription drugs, the following links are available:

http://www.healthtouch.com

http://www.rxlist.com

Expert witnesses

Most cases involving personal injuries require expert witnesses. In addition to the usual medical experts, any number of others may be required. Sites that provide links to experts of all kinds are available at:

http://www.expertpages.com

http://www.expertlaw.com

Damages

One of the most important aspects of the civil suit is the assessment and evaluation of damages. The Internet provides sites that show data from lawsuits that have been previously settled. One site is located at:

http://www.ljextra.com/cgi-bin/vds

The Kelley Blue Book site provides data on the value of automobiles and is located at:

http://www.kbb.com

REAL PROPERTY LAW

The area of real property law involves a number of different specialties, including real estate sales, litigation over real estate transactions, and landlord/tenant issues. In some states, real estate sales transactions utilize escrow companies to complete a sale, while in others, law firms complete this process in what is known as a "closing."

Real Estate Transactions

The Real Estate Transaction Network provides a method for conducting real estate transactions online. Their Data Track Systems offer links with real estate companies, mortgage providers, title companies, and real estate appraisers enabling a rapid transfer of information for real estate sales. Their site is located at:

http://www.datatrac.com

The National Association of Realtors maintains its own site at:

http://www.realtor.com

In addition to providing over 400,000 properties for sale in most states, it also offers links to information concerning the value of real estate.

A site of interest to those dealing in international properties are located at:

http://www.fiabci-usa.com

and

http://www.estate.de

The California Association of Realtors has developed a particularly noteworthy site at:

http://www.car.org

This site provides the largest source listing of California properties on the Internet. It also has links to continuing education and professional development sites in real estate, legislative information, news, research, economics, legal resources online for real estate matters, and many other links of note.

For individuals involved in the commercial real estate market, the Commercial Real Estate Network is maintained by the Certified Commercial Investment Members (CCIM) organization, which is dedicated to facilitating networking and information sharing among its members and the general public. CCIM is a professional organization for those in commercial real estate brokerage, asset management, valuation, investment analysis, and leasing. The site provides market trends in commercial real estate, discussion forums, and a calendar of events of the organization. The site is located at:

http://www.ccim.com

A listing of real estate appraisers by state may be found at:

http://www.inrealty.com/ss/frm-subj.html

This site also provides resources related to appraisals, accounting, brokerage, demographics, economics, finance, insurance, taxation, law, and management.

Information on state licensing requirements as well as how to contact the states' real estate commissions and regulatory agencies is located at:

http://www.real-estate-ed.com/docs/usmap.htm

Landlord/Tenant Issues

Nolo Press, a self-help legal book publisher in California, maintains a site listing articles on landlord/tenant law, issues involving neighbors and homeowners, and neighborhoods and safety, at:

http://www.nolo.com/home.html

Additional information about landlord/tenant law is available on individual lawyers' home pages. It is important to always determine when the page was last updated to be sure to obtain the latest laws and rulings.

TAX LAW

Attorneys who practice in tax law must be familiar with the tax laws of the federal government as well as their individual states. The federal regulations on taxes are available on the following sites:

1. Virtual Law Library—**http://www.law.indiana.edu/law/v-lib. taxes.html**
   This site provides several links to a number of different sources in tax law.

2. Internal Revenue Service—**http://www.irs.ustreas.gov/**
   The IRS site provides information about where to file taxes, how to get assistance, tax forms, and instructions for forms completion.

3. United States Tax Code—**http://www.law.cornell.edu/uscode/26/** and **http://www.tns.lcs.mit.edu/uscode/**   (Key word searches)

A few sites provide information on both state and federal tax regulations. Among the more comprehensive sites is:

http://www.best.com:80/%/7Eftmexpat/html/taxsites.html

In addition to providing documents and forms for federal taxes, this site provides links to newsgroups, tax articles, legislative and judicial resources, tax treaties, state tax laws, social security information, and foreign tax codes.

One site that provides a number of links to both federal and state tax law sites is located at:

http://www.el.com/ToTheWeb/Taxes/

⊕ ASSIGNMENTS

1. Find the Bankruptcy Court in the closest metropolitan area to your home. Put its web address here. _____

2. Does your state have a Lemon Law? _____ Describe the contents of this law. _____

   _____

   List the web page on which this law was found: _____

3. Is there an agency in your state for the protection of the environment? If so, list the name of the agency and the address of its web page. If not, provide the web address for the Environmental Protection Agency.

    _____

    _____

    _____

4. How can a Canadian citizen get a green card for employment and entry into the United States? _____

    _____

5. Does your state's Secretary of State's Office have a web page? If so, list its address. _____

    Does the web page provide forms for drafting Articles of Incorporation? _____ If so, provide one here. _____

6. Does your state have a state income tax? _____ List the web page for your state's tax laws . _____

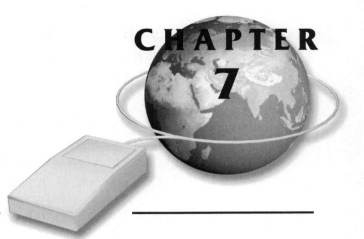

CHAPTER
7

International
Law

In addition to using the previously discussed law libraries to find information about international law, a number of other sites are available as well. This area of law is generally involved with legal relationships and interactions between different countries, or legal relations between individuals or corporations from different countries. It also involves international trade agreements, treaties, and contracts.

A number of countries have their constitutions available online, including those listed below:

1. Latin-American countries (in Spanish)—
   http://161.132.29.12/CCD/constitucion/constitucion.html

2. Australia, European countries, Canada, Mexico—
   http://www.ukans.edu/carrie/docs/docscon.html

3. Worldwide Constitutions (many countries)—
   http://www.eur.nl/iacl/const.html

4. Many countries' constitutions along with other material on constitutional law in these countries—
   http://www.law.cornell.edu/law/index.html

Many countries have their laws online, as well as trade agreements and treaties, along with links to branches of their governments. Included in this list are the following:

1. British Parliament—
   http://www.hmsoinfo.gov.uk/hmso/document/Acts.htm
2. Australia—**http://austlii.law.uts.edu.au/**
3. Japan—**http://home.highway.or.jp/JAPANLAW/index.htm**
4. Canada

   A. Copyright—**http://cancopy.com**
   B. Legal links—
      http://www.law.ubc.ca/links/bowers/bowers.html
   C. Law sources—**http://gahtan.com/lawlinks/**

5. France—**http://www.fdn.fr/~rabenou/index.html**

The Library of Congress maintains a site for the Global Legal Information Network and provides a database of laws from countries all over the world. It is often the best place to start when doing research into international law and is available at:

http://lcweb2.loc.gov/glin/glinhome.html

The World Court maintains a web site at:

http://www.law.cornell.edu/icj

The Court, also known as the International Court of Justice, is the supreme judicial body of the United Nations. The following materials are available on this site:

1. Statutes
2. Treaties
3. Decisions
4. Advisory opinions
5. United Nations charter
6. News about the United Nations
7. Students' resources
8. International law websites

⊕ ASSIGNMENTS

1. Look up a case that has been decided in the World Court. Prepare a case brief and include the following information therein:
   A. Case name
   B. Citation
   C. Brief statement of the facts, including countries involved in case
   D. Issue being decided
   E. Rule of law
   F. Court's decision and rationale

2. Does the World Court hold sessions online? If so describe how this is accomplished. Where did you find this information? _____

   _____

3. What is the punishment in Japan for murder? What is the code section and address of the web page where you found this information?

   _____

   _____

Law Firms and Professional Organizations

Many private attorneys and law firms have their own web pages. The best way to find a specific law firm's web page is to do a search using the name of the firm in quotation marks. Using one of the search engines described in Chapter 1, key the name of the law firm within quotation marks into the search box. If that firm has a web page, its location should show upon the search engine's results page. If you are not certain of the firm's full name, then key in the name as you think it is without the quotation marks. For example, if you know the name of the firm, you might key:

"Long Law Firm"

but if you are not sure of the name of the firm, you would key:

Long Law Firm

WEST LEGAL DIRECTORY

The *West Legal Directory* represents biographical listings of over 800,000 lawyers. Searches are possible by subject, practice area, attributes of the attorney, and location. For example, it would be possible to search for "a Spanish-speaking immigration attorney in Los Angeles." It is possible to search the following subjects in the *West Legal Directory,* accessible at:

http://www.lawoffice.com

1. Search by name

2. United States lawyers

3. International counsel

4. Corporate lawyers

5. Government lawyers

6. United States courts

7. Law students

8. Lawyer services guides

9. Areas of law

10. State law information

11. Overview of the United States courts

12. Law dictionary

13. Articles from different law firms

14. How to hire a lawyer

In addition, each day certain articles from law firms are featured by provided links. Figure 8-1 is the home page of the *West Legal Directory*.

A locator service for attorneys can be found at:

http://www.attorneyfind.com/

This site enables you to search for law firms and lawyers in different states and different specialty areas.

Most people who have worked in law offices are familiar with the *Martindale-Hubbell Legal Directory of Attorneys and Law Firms*. This same directory is now provided online at:

http://www.martindale.com

There are over 900,000 listings in this directory of law firms and attorneys in the United States and other parts of the world. Searches are possible by name, city, state, country, language, and province. It is also possible to search here for government attorneys and corporate law departments. Individual listings for attorneys include their name, address, telephone number, areas of practice, educational background, professional affiliations, and sometimes representative clients.

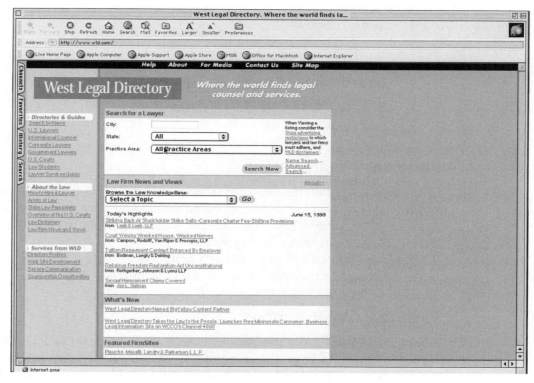

FIGURE 8-1   West Legal Directory home page

PROFESSIONAL ORGANIZATIONS

American Bar Association

The American Bar Association (ABA) maintains its web site at:

http://www.abanet.org/

In addition to providing information about the organization for its members, a considerable number of other items are also included on the site:

1. Membership information
2. Publications of the ABA
3. Continuing legal education issues

4. The *ABA Journal*
5. Links to other law-related sites
6. Information about the legal community
7. Public information about the legal profession
8. Specialty sections and news about their events
9. Paralegal information

State Bar Organizations

Space does not permit the listing of all state bar organizations in the country. However, a search may be conducted to find your own state's bar organization by doing a key word search. When you establish the search engine, key into the space for key words:

"Indiana State Bar"   or   Indiana State Bar

or whatever state's bar organization is the object of your research.

Paralegal Organizations

A number of paralegal organizations exist both on the local and national level. Probably the largest local paralegal organization in the country is the Los Angeles Paralegal Association (LAPA), with 1,100 members in the greater Los Angeles metropolitan region. Its site can be found at:

http://www.lapa.org

The organization is dedicated to the development of the paralegal profession and provides opportunities for professional development and networking. The site maintains information about meetings and upcoming events. It also has links to monthly publication information, member benefits, specialty groups, and specialty services for members, including a resume bank for job searching, membership directory, annual employment and salary survey, paralegal schools list, and a job hunting handbook. Students may join LAPA for a reduced fee.

The National Association for Legal Assistants (NALA) is a leading national professional association for paralegals; its site may be found at:

http://www.nala.org

The Association provides continuing education and professional certification programs for paralegals. NALA was incorporated in 1975 and is one of the oldest paralegal organizations in the United States. The site contains information about its quarterly journal, *Facts and Findings*. It also provides an online campus, with classes and seminars offered. The Internet campus was developed by West Publishing Company and NALA for legal professionals. Classes are available for the Certified Legal Assistant examination, continuing legal education, and paralegal skills. Classes presently offered include Communications, Judgment and Legal Analysis, and Legal Research.

This site also provides links to vendors and other professional legal organizations, including:

1. American Law Institute-American Bar Association Committee
2. Association of Legal Administrators
3. American Association for Paralegal Education (paralegal educators)
4. Corporate Law Department
5. National Notary Association
6. Legal Assistants Division of the State Bar of Texas

A link is provided to the *American Standard Dictionary,* and to Information America, which searches public records free or for a nominal fee.

Another national organization in the paralegal area is the National Federation of Paralegal Associations (NFPA) located at:

http://www.paralegals.org

which is their main web page, and contains another page that provides links to state and federal statutes as well as many other sites of interest to paralegals, located at:

http://www.paralegals.org/LegalResources.home.html

NFPA's main web page provides links to press releases, surveys, news, legal research sources, products, services, calendar, career center for paralegals, articles on getting started in the paralegal profession, membership information, *National Paralegal Reporter* publication, professional development, paralegal advanced competency examination, networking (listservs and chat rooms), publications, international information, continuing legal education online, *pro bono* activities and opportunities in the field.

Their legal research links include:

1. Federal agencies
2. Federal departments

3. Federal statutes and cases
4. State agencies and departments
5. State statutes and cases
6. State and federal courts
7. International law
8. Internet directories and search engines
9. Sites for specialty practice
10. Organization and association links
11. Listservs and law-related forums
12. Law schools and research centers

They maintain seventeen listservs, most of which are for members only, including:

1. Bankruptcy/collections
2. Corporate law
3. Corporate litigation department paralegals
4. Criminal law
5. Educators
6. Family law
7. Freelance paralegals
8. General discussion
9. Immigration
10. Labor law
11. Law office management
12. Litigation
13. Independent paralegals
14. Intellectual property
15. Probate, estates and trusts
16. Real estate law
17. Students
18. Technology

The American Association for Paralegal Education (AAfPE) is a national organization that serves paralegal education and institutions offering paralegal education programs. Its site, located at:

http://www.aafpe.org

includes information on paralegal programs throughout the country, as well as membership, educational resources, association links, and news for paralegal educators. It contains articles from the *Journal*. An Internet discussion list and a list of state bar associations and publishers are provided. The page contains an article on how to choose a paralegal program. A searchable membership directory is provided, with e-mail links to program directors at member colleges and universities.

The Association of Legal Administrators (ALA) provides its web site at:

http://www.alanet.org/

This group's mission is to improve the quality of management in legal services organizations; promote and enhance the competence and professionalism of legal administrators and management; and represent professional legal management in the community.[3]

Some items on this site are available to members of the organization only:

1. Links to annual education conference
2. Association news
3. Career information
4. Industry digests
5. Available documents
6. Online discussion group
7. Continuing professional education
8. Association and legal management industry news
9. Membership information

Many law office employees also become Notary Publics. The web site for the National Notary Association is located at:

http://www.nna.org

---

3 Association of Legal Administrators' Web Page; home page; **http://www.alanet.org/**.

The National Association of Legal Secretaries (NALS) has a national office and branches throughout the country. Their main site is located at:

http://www.nals.org/

Their web page has links to other legal resources, membership information, legal news applicable to legal secretaries, a chat room, and a description of the advantages and benefits of their organization. Some state branches also have their own web sites.

COLLEGES

Most colleges throughout the United States offer pre-law, paralegal, and legal secretarial programs. Information and recommendations about different programs may be obtained from your state bar association, the site for the American Association for Paralegal Education, the National Association of Legal Assistants, and the National Association of Legal Secretaries. All of these web sites are discussed above.

Law schools have been discussed in a previous chapter and their web sites noted. Investigate the ABA site and your State Bar Association's site for information on choosing a law school. The ABA also has a section for legal assistants (paralegals) that approves paralegal programs throughout the country. Information about this procedure may be found on their site.

Many local and statewide professional organizations exist in the legal area and are too numerous to completely list here. However, you now have the tools to search the Internet to find the types of schools that would be of interest to you.

⊕ ASSIGNMENTS

1. Find the web site for the state bar association in your state. What is its web site address? _____

2. Do a search for a law firm in your town that has a web site and specializes in criminal law. What is its name and what is its web address?

   _____

   _____

3. What professional organizations exist on a national level for attorneys? Where are their web sites found? _____

4. Does the National Association of Legal Secretaries have a branch in the county in which you live? _____ Do they have a web site? _____ Give the web site address. _____

5. Is there a local paralegal association in the metropolitan area nearest to where you live? _____ What is its web site address? _____

6. Describe the professional organizations that would be of benefit to you in your future career and why. _____

_____